TEACHER'S EDITION

TEST BEST

ON THE
IOWA
TESTS OF
BASIC SKILLS®

LEVEL 11

STECK-VAUGHN
C O M P A N Y

A Division of Harcourt Brace & Company

www.steck-vaughn.com

Acknowledgments

Executive Editor: Diane Sharpe
Project Editor: Janet Jerzycki
Editor: Amanda Johnson
Contributing Author: Jay Comras
Graphics Project Manager: Sheryl Bankford
Production: Go Media, Inc., Austin, Texas
Cover Design: D Childress/Alan Klemp
Illustrators: Sonya Cohen, Holly Cooper, Julie Gomoll, John Hartwell, Gwendolyn Manney, Rachel Matthews, Kay Wilson

Pronunciation key reproduced with permission of Macmillan/McGraw-Hill School Publishing Company from *Macmillan School Dictionary 1* (ISBN 0-02-195003-2) *Grade 3-5* and *Macmillan School Dictionary 2* (ISBN 0-02-195004-0) *Grade 6-8.* Copyright © 1990.

Test Best is a registered trademark of Steck-Vaughn Company.

Iowa Tests of Basic Skills® is a trademark of The Riverside Publishing Company. Such company has neither endorsed nor authorized this test-preparation book.

Contents

Test Best on the Iowa Tests of Basic Skills has been developed to refresh basic skills, familiarize students with test formats and directions, and to teach test-taking strategies for the Iowa Tests of Basic Skills. *Test Best* provides teachers with materials to ensure that students take the test under optimal conditions—that test-wise students be able to concentrate on what they know without being overwhelmed by a testing situation with which they are unfamiliar.

Being well-prepared for a test means knowing how to approach different types of questions and how to use time wisely. By using the *Test Best* books prior to the administration of the Iowa Tests of Basic Skills, students will learn such skills, as well as be able to control their anxiety about a test and to keep their concentration high throughout the testing period. Armed with the skills they have learned as they work through *Test Best on the Iowa Tests of Basic Skills*, students can truly perform well.

The Steck-Vaughn *Test Best* Series for Grades K–8

Test Best on the Iowa Tests of Basic Skills consists of nine student books. You will need to determine which book is best suited to the abilities and needs of your students. The series is organized as follows:

Book	Grade Levels
Level 5	Kindergarten
Levels 6–7	Grade 1
Level 8	Grade 2
Level 9	Grade 3
Level 10	Grade 4
Level 11	Grade 5
Level 12	Grade 6
Level 13	Grade 7
Level 14	Grade 8

Objectives of the Series

To Increase Awareness of Test-Taking Strategies

Test-taking strategies should focus on three important test principles:
1. Time Use
   - Not spending too much time on any one question
   - Working rapidly but comfortably
   - Marking items to return to if time permits
   - Using any time remaining to review answers
   - Using a watch (at the appropriate age) to keep track of time
2. Error Avoidance
   - Paying careful attention to directions
   - Determining clearly what is being asked
   - Marking answers in the appropriate place
   - Checking all answers
   - Being neat by not making stray marks on the answer sheet
3. Reasoning
   - Reading the entire question or passage and all the choices before answering a question
   - Applying what has been learned

To Increase Awareness of Directions

It is important that students understand the directions for taking the tests. Therefore, one of the key objectives of the program is to familiarize students with directions. Doing so builds self-confidence and permits students to utilize their time more effectively.

To Increase Awareness of Content and Skills

Anxiety often results from a lack of information about the knowledge and skills the tests will cover. You and your students will find that increased awareness of content and skills are significant outcomes of the program.

To Increase Awareness of Format

By practicing the skills needed to meet your school's educational objectives, the students will be gaining invaluable experience with test formats. Such familiarity permits students to spend more time applying what they have learned.

To Understand How the Test Is Administered

Students are sometimes uncomfortable anticipating what will happen on the day of the tests. Becoming familiar with the procedures, directions, and the process of test taking helps reduce anxiety and uncertainty.

Format of the Books

Each of the nine student books is divided into units that correspond to those found in the Iowa Tests of Basic Skills. The units vary but can include Vocabulary, Word Analysis, Listening, Reading Comprehension, Spelling, Language Mechanics, Language Expression, Math Concepts and Estimation, Math Problems, Math Computation, Maps and Diagrams, and Reference Materials. Within each of these units are the skills covered on the tests.

Each skill lesson generally includes:

Directions—clear, concise, and similar to those found in the Iowa Tests of Basic Skills;

Try This— a skill strategy for students that enables them to approach each lesson exercise in a logical manner;

A Sample—to familiarize students with test-taking items;

Think It Through—a specific explanation to students of the correct answer in the Sample item that tells why the incorrect answers are wrong and why the correct answer is correct;

A Practice Section—a set of exercises based on the lesson and modeled on the kinds of exercises found in the Iowa Tests of Basic Skills.

Each unit is followed by a Unit Test that covers all the skills in the unit lessons and affords students the opportunity to experience a situation close to the testing situation. Each book concludes with a series of Comprehensive Tests—one for each unit covered in the book. The *Test Best Comprehensive Tests* give students an opportunity to take a test under conditions that parallel those they will face when taking the Iowa Tests of Basic Skills.

The Teacher's Edition

The Teacher's Edition of *Test Best on the Iowa Tests of Basic Skills* contains a Scope and Sequence and reduced student pages complete with answers. The Teacher's Edition also provides a detailed plan of action and suggestions for teaching and administering each of the lessons and tests, including the Sample items. Scripts are provided so that students become familiar with the oral directions given on the tests themselves.

Also contained in the Teacher's Edition is an introductory lesson designed to acquaint students with the *Test Best on the Iowa Tests of Basic Skills* program. This lesson appears on pages 7 through 10 and should be used before beginning Lesson 1 with students.

Scope and Sequence

READING COMPREHENSION SKILLS

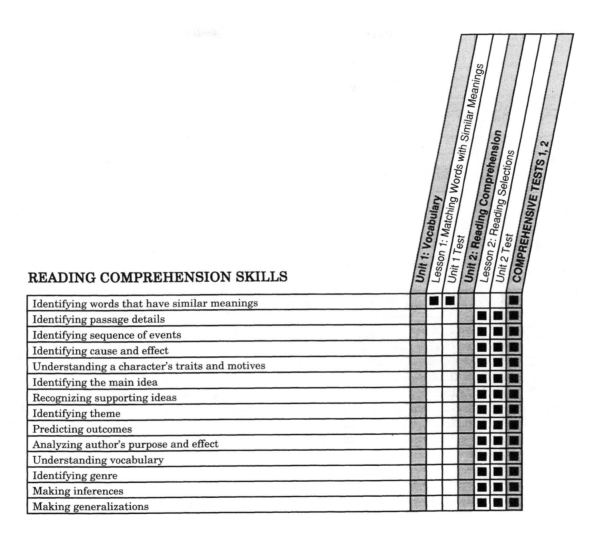

	Unit 1: Vocabulary	Lesson 1: Matching Words with Similar Meanings	Unit 1 Test	Unit 2: Reading Comprehension	Lesson 2: Reading Selections	Unit 2 Test	COMPREHENSIVE TESTS 1, 2
Identifying words that have similar meanings		■	■				■
Identifying passage details					■	■	■
Identifying sequence of events					■	■	■
Identifying cause and effect					■	■	■
Understanding a character's traits and motives					■	■	■
Identifying the main idea					■	■	■
Recognizing supporting ideas					■	■	■
Identifying theme					■	■	■
Predicting outcomes					■	■	■
Analyzing author's purpose and effect					■	■	■
Understanding vocabulary					■	■	■
Identifying genre					■	■	■
Making inferences					■	■	■
Making generalizations					■	■	■

LANGUAGE SKILLS

Language Skills	Unit 3: Spelling	Lesson 3: Checking Word Spellings	Unit 3 Test	Unit 4: Language Mechanics	Lesson 4: Using Correct Capitalization	Lesson 5: Using Correct Punctuation	Unit 4 Test	Unit 5: Language Expression	Lesson 6: Determining Usage	Lesson 7: Choosing Correct Words and Phrases	Lesson 8: Analyzing Paragraphs	Lesson 9: Expressing Ideas Clearly	Unit 5 Test	COMPREHENSIVE TESTS 3, 4, 5
Identifying correct spellings of words		■	■											■
Recognizing misspelled words		■	■											■
Identifying the need for capitalization in sentences					■		■							■
Identifying the need for punctuation in sentences						■	■							■
Determining the appropriate use of nouns, verbs, adjectives, and adverbs within the context of sentences									■				■	■
Identifying words and phrases that best fit in the context of a sentence										■			■	■
Determining the topic and supporting details of a paragraph											■		■	■
Identifying information that does not belong in a paragraph											■		■	■
Determining word usage in the context of a paragraph											■		■	■
Identifying sentences that are the clearest, most concise, and best examples of effective writing												■	■	■

Scope and Sequence

MATHEMATICS SKILLS

Mathematics Skills	Unit 6: Math Concepts and Estimation	Lesson 10: Understanding Numeration	Lesson 11: Working with Number Sentences	Lesson 12: Using Probability and Statistics	Lesson 13: Using Measurement and Geometry	Lesson 14: Using Estimation	Unit 6 Test	Unit 7: Math Problems	Lesson 15: Solving Problems	Lesson 16: Working with Graphs	Unit 7 Test	Unit 8: Math Computation	Lesson 17: Adding	Lesson 18: Subtracting	Lesson 19: Multiplying	Lesson 20: Dividing	Unit 8 Test	COMPREHENSIVE TESTS 6, 7, 8
Identifying place value, fractional parts, and multiples of numbers		■					■											■
Estimating		■				■	■											■
Understanding number theory and relationships		■					■											■
Solving number sentences			■				■											■
Understanding probability and statistics concepts				■			■											■
Applying probability and statistics concepts in problem solving				■			■											■
Working with customary and metric units of length, quantity, height, and weight					■		■											■
Identifying congruent and similar figures					■		■											■
Determining time, area, and perimeter of plane figures					■		■											■
Recognizing three-dimensional forms					■		■											■
Identifying angles and line segments					■		■											■
Solving one-step and multiple-step word problems									■		■							■
Analyzing graphs										■	■							■
Evaluating graphic displays and using the information to solve problems										■	■							■
Adding whole numbers, decimals, fractions, and mixed numbers													■				■	■
Subtracting whole numbers, decimals, fractions, and mixed numbers														■			■	■
Multiplying whole numbers															■		■	■
Dividing whole numbers																■	■	■

STUDY SKILLS

Skill	Unit 9: Maps and Diagrams	Lesson 21: Working with Maps	Lesson 22: Working with Charts and Diagrams	Unit 9 Test	Unit 10: Reference Materials	Lesson 23: Using a Table of Contents	Lesson 24: Alphabetizing	Lesson 25: Using Reference Materials	Lesson 26: Using the Dictionary	Lesson 27: Using the Library	Unit 10 Test	COMPREHENSIVE TESTS 9, 10
Using map symbols and keys to describe and locate places		■		■								■
Determining direction and distance		■		■								■
Interpreting data on population, transportation, production, elevation, and resources		■		■								■
Tracing travel routes		■		■								■
Interpreting information in schedules, charts, tables, and diagrams			■	■								■
Using a table of contents to find and determine information						■					■	■
Alphabetizing beyond the first letter of a given word							■				■	■
Identifying the appropriate encyclopedia volume to use to locate specific information								■			■	■
Obtaining information by interpreting dictionary entries									■		■	■
Choosing appropriate reference materials to gather specific information										■	■	■
Using a card catalog										■	■	■

Introducing Students to *Test Best*

Use this orientation lesson to familiarize students with the format of *Test Best on the Iowa Tests of Basic Skills*, Level 11, and with steps for preparing for and taking the Iowa Tests of Basic Skills.

SAY: At certain times during the school year, you may take one or more achievement tests. These tests show how well you are doing in certain subjects, compared to other students of your age group across the country.

Discuss test taking and how students feel about taking standardized tests.

SAY: Do you remember the last time you took achievement tests? Were you nervous? Were you worried? How did you feel when you finished the tests? Do you think you did your best on the tests?

Point out to students that most people worry when they have to take a test. Explain that *Test Best* practice lessons and class discussions can help reduce anxiety and help increase confidence.

SAY: Try not to worry about achievement tests. These tests will not affect your school grades. Instead, the achievement tests will tell you some interesting things about yourself—about the skills you have mastered and the skills you need to learn.

Distribute the *Test Best* books to students. Tell students that *Test Best* will familiarize them with the kinds of questions on the Iowa Tests of Basic Skills and how it feels to take this kind of test.

SAY: Some test items will be more difficult than others. Some material may be new to you. But that's all right. You will be given enough time to work on each test.

Allow students to skim through the books for a minute or two.

SAY: Now we will look at one of the lessons. Turn to Lesson 1 on page 1. Put your finger on the Directions.

Explain that each lesson begins with a set of Directions. Ask students why it is important to read and follow directions when taking tests.

UNIT 1 Vocabulary

Lesson 1: Matching Words with Similar Meanings

Directions: Darken the circle for the word or words that mean the <u>same</u> or <u>almost the same</u> as the word in dark type.

> **TRY THIS**
> Read the phrase. Think about the meaning of the word in dark type. Sometimes you can get a hint about the meaning of the word in dark type by studying the whole phrase. Be careful not to choose a word or words that mean the opposite of the word in dark type.

S1 Whistle a pretty **melody**
A tune
B dress
C bird
D picture

> **THINK IT THROUGH**
> The correct answer is A. Tune is closest in meaning to <u>melody</u>. Dress, <u>bird</u>, and picture may make sense with the word <u>pretty</u>, but they do not make sense with the word <u>melody</u>.

STOP

---

1 To **accept** payment
A disagree with
B pass over
C agree to take
D turn down

2 Located at a high **altitude**
J height
K opinion
L answer
M country

3 Very **dense** woods
A stringy
B hollow
C rough
D thick

4 To firmly **declare** his loyalty
J press
K pack
L state
M insist

5 To **bitterly** regret her actions
A angrily
B rarely
C happily
D hopefully

6 An **advocate** of free trade
J trainee
K supporter
L polluter
M merchant

7 Become quite **furious**
A impatient
B amused
C calm
D angry

8 A **gala** event
J joyous
K frequent
L giant
M spoiled

9 A **hint** of spring
A parade
B trace
C trick
D champion

STOP

Answers
S1 ● Ⓑ Ⓒ Ⓓ   2 Ⓙ ● Ⓛ Ⓜ   4 Ⓙ Ⓚ ● Ⓜ   6 Ⓙ ● Ⓛ Ⓜ   8 ● Ⓚ Ⓛ Ⓜ
1 Ⓐ Ⓑ ● Ⓓ   3 Ⓐ Ⓑ Ⓒ ●   5 ● Ⓑ Ⓒ Ⓓ   7 Ⓐ Ⓑ Ⓒ ●   9 Ⓐ ● Ⓒ Ⓓ

Level 11

1

UNIT 1 Vocabulary

Lesson 1: Matching Words with Similar Meanings

Directions: Darken the circle for the word or words that mean the <u>same</u> or <u>almost the same</u> as the word in dark type.

| TRY THIS | Read the phrase. Think about the meaning of the word in dark type. Sometimes you can get a hint about the meaning of the word in dark type by studying the whole phrase. Be careful not to choose a word or words that mean the opposite of the word in dark type. |

S1   Whistle a pretty **melody**

    A tune

    B dress

    C bird

    D picture

 | THINK IT THROUGH | The correct answer is A. Tune is closest in meaning to <u>melody</u>. Dress, bird, and picture may make sense with the word <u>pretty</u>, but they do not make sense with the word <u>melody</u>.

STOP

---

1   To **accept** payment

    A disagree with

    B pass over

    C agree to take

    D turn down

2   Located at a high **altitude**

    J height

    K opinion

    L answer

    M country

3   Very **dense** woods

    A stringy

    B hollow

    C rough

    D thick

4   To firmly **declare** his loyalty

    J press

    K pack

    L state

    M insist

5   To **bitterly** regret her actions

    A angrily

    B rarely

    C happily

    D hopefully

6   An **advocate** of free trade

    J trainee

    K supporter

    L polluter

    M merchant

7   Become quite **furious**

    A impatient

    B amused

    C calm

    D angry

8   A **gala** event

    J joyous

    K frequent

    L giant

    M spoiled

9   A **hint** of spring

    A parade

    B trace

    C trick

    D champion

STOP

Answers

Level 11

S1 ● Ⓑ Ⓒ Ⓓ   2 ● Ⓚ Ⓛ Ⓜ   4 Ⓙ Ⓚ ● Ⓜ   6 Ⓙ ● Ⓛ Ⓜ   8 ● Ⓚ Ⓛ Ⓜ

1 Ⓐ Ⓑ ● Ⓓ   3 Ⓐ Ⓑ Ⓒ ●   5 ● Ⓑ Ⓒ Ⓓ   7 Ⓐ Ⓑ Ⓒ ●   9 Ⓐ ● Ⓒ Ⓓ

1

SAY: **Find the <u>Try This</u> section. Let's read this section together. <u>Try This</u> suggests a way to answer the question. There are other ways to figure the answer to a question. <u>Try This</u> offers one way. Now look at the <u>Sample</u> below <u>Try This</u>. We will always work through the <u>Samples</u> together before you work the practice exercises on your own.**

Copy the <u>Sample</u> onto the chalkboard. Work through the <u>Sample</u> orally with students, and demonstrate the proper way to darken the answer spaces. Explain to students the importance of filling the answer space, pressing firmly on the pencil to make a dark mark, and erasing any stray marks that might be picked up as answers by the scoring machines.

SAY: **Now find <u>Think It Through</u>. <u>Think It Through</u> is an explanation of the best answer. <u>Think It Through</u> usually explains why the other choices are wrong.**

Ask students if they have any questions about the lesson features up to this point.

SAY: **What do you see below <u>Think It Through</u>? (The word *STOP*) What should you do when you see the word *STOP*? (Stop what you are doing.)**

Tell students that they will see the word *STOP* throughout the lessons and on the Iowa Tests of Basic Skills. Explain that the word *STOP* tells students to stop what they are doing, put their pencils down, and wait for further instructions from the teacher.

SAY: **What do you see below <u>Think It Through</u> and the word *STOP*? (Numbered exercises) Each lesson has a practice section with exercises.**

Unit 1 Test

S1 To feel **drowsy**
A alert
B cold
C confused
D sleepy

STOP

For questions 1–13, darken the circle for the word or words that mean the same or almost the same as the word in dark type.

1 To pay **homage**
A honor
B bearer
C spite
D guaranty

2 An interesting **comment**
J remark
K image
L completion
M story

3 To **simultaneously** link the stations
A one at a time
B using lasers
C with advanced technology
D at the same time

4 A **meek** office manager
J easily imposed upon
K arrogant
L loud-speaking
M artistic

5 A **graceful** dancer
A tall
B young
C awkward
D elegant

6 To **latch** the door
J beat
K fasten
L open
M paint

7 To **mock** someone's beliefs
A praise
B defy
C ridicule
D puzzle

8 Require an immediate **response**
J trial
K answer
L reward
M apology

9 A **stationary** weather front
A life-threatening
B unusual
C not moving
D approaching

10 To **lodge** a complaint
J discourage
K repeat
L celebrate
M file

11 To **desire** something
A claim
B suspend
C want
D repeat

12 To **achieve** a goal
J go after
K reach
L say no to
M search for

13 Appear **meticulously** groomed
A sloppily
B without shoes
C very carefully
D out-of-fashion

STOP

Answers
S1 Ⓐ Ⓑ Ⓒ ●
1 ● Ⓑ Ⓒ Ⓓ
2 ● Ⓚ Ⓛ Ⓜ
3 Ⓐ Ⓑ Ⓒ ●
4 ● Ⓚ Ⓛ Ⓜ
5 Ⓐ Ⓑ Ⓒ ●
6 Ⓙ ● Ⓛ Ⓜ
7 Ⓐ Ⓑ ● Ⓓ
8 Ⓙ ● Ⓛ Ⓜ
9 Ⓐ Ⓑ ● Ⓓ
10 Ⓙ Ⓚ Ⓛ ●
11 Ⓐ Ⓑ ● Ⓓ
12 Ⓙ ● Ⓛ Ⓜ
13 Ⓐ Ⓑ ● Ⓓ

Level 11

2

Have students turn to the Unit 1 Test on page 2. Explain that there is a unit test at the end of each unit that gives students an opportunity to practice taking a test. Have students locate the <u>Sample</u> at the beginning of the test. Tell students that you will always work the <u>Sample</u> together as a class before they work the rest of the test. Explain that this test will include the skills practiced in the unit lessons.

Ask students if they have any questions about the lessons or the unit tests. Explain that (at the end of the book) there are Comprehensive Tests.

Comprehensive Tests

Test 1: Vocabulary

S1 Raw vegetables
- A uncooked
- B crunchy
- C sliced
- D pickled

STOP

For questions 1–28, darken the circle for the word or words that mean the <u>same</u> or <u>almost the same</u> as the word <u>in dark type</u>.

1 A ridiculous suggestion
- A thoughtless
- B sharp
- C foolish
- D serious

2 To show great astonishment
- J fear
- K happiness
- L surprise
- M hope

3 To nestle
- A snuggle
- B irritate
- C organize
- D misjudge

4 Offered a vague explanation
- J uncertain
- K cautious
- L capable
- M clear

5 To gain respect
- A fill
- B lose
- C change
- D earn

6 Signed a peace pact
- J stake
- K paper
- L agreement
- M sketch

7 Regarded as an outcast
- A displaced person
- B aftereffect
- C nozzle
- D old person

8 Delivered an accurate report
- J correct
- K exaggerated
- L incorrect
- M reliable

9 The outskirts of town
- A exterior
- B border
- C center
- D ledge

10 Snug clothing
- J cotton
- K warm
- L tight
- M loose

11 To live in miserable poverty
- A delighted
- B concerned
- C unhappy
- D angry

12 To be a pacifist
- J easily alarmed person
- K hateful person
- L careful person
- M peaceable person

13 Opposing the idea
- A supporting
- B voting against
- C making up
- D covering up

GO ON

Level 11

SAY: **Turn to page 65. Read the title at the top of the page.** (*Comprehensive Tests, Test 1: Vocabulary*) **There are ten Comprehensive Tests—one test for each unit in the book. When we take the Comprehensive Tests, we will follow the test conditions that will be used during the Iowa Tests of Basic Skills. For example, I will provide you with sharpened pencils and scratch paper for the mathematics tests. Also, each test will have a time limit. The Comprehensive Tests will give you a final chance to apply the skills that you practiced in the lessons in** *Test Best* **before you take the Iowa Tests of Basic Skills.**

What do you see at the bottom of page 65? (The words *GO ON.*) **These words tell you to turn to the next page and continue working.**

Explain to students that the words *GO ON* will appear in some two-page lessons, in most unit tests, and in the comprehensive tests.

Ask students if they have any questions about the Comprehensive Tests.

SAY: **When you take the Iowa Tests of Basic Skills, you may feel a little nervous at first. Try to remember what you have learned in** *Test Best* **about taking tests. You will be able to use what you have learned in your classes, too. Then you should be ready to do your very best.**

UNIT 1 Vocabulary

Lesson 1: Matching Words with Similar Meanings

Directions: Darken the circle for the word or words that mean the <u>same</u> or <u>almost the same</u> as the word in dark type.

TRY THIS	Read the phrase. Think about the meaning of the word in dark type. Sometimes you can get a hint about the meaning of the word in dark type by studying the whole phrase. Be careful not to choose a word or words that mean the opposite of the word in dark type.

S1 Whistle a pretty **melody**

A tune
B dress
C bird
D picture

THINK IT THROUGH	The correct answer is A. Tune is closest in meaning to melody. Dress, bird, and picture may make sense with the word pretty, but they do not make sense with the word melody.

STOP

1 To **accept** payment
A disagree with
B pass over
C agree to take
D turn down

2 Located at a high **altitude**
J height
K opinion
L answer
M country

3 Very **dense** woods
A stringy
B hollow
C rough
D thick

4 To firmly **declare** his loyalty
J press
K pack
L state
M insist

5 To **bitterly** regret her actions
A angrily
B rarely
C happily
D hopefully

6 An **advocate** of free trade
J trainee
K supporter
L polluter
M merchant

7 Become quite **furious**
A impatient
B amused
C calm
D angry

8 A **gala** event
J joyous
K frequent
L giant
M spoiled

9 A **hint** of spring
A parade
B trace
C trick
D champion

STOP

Level 11

Answers
S1 ● Ⓑ Ⓒ Ⓓ   2 ● Ⓚ Ⓛ Ⓜ   4 Ⓙ Ⓚ ● Ⓜ   6 Ⓙ ● Ⓛ Ⓜ   8 ● Ⓚ Ⓛ Ⓜ
1 Ⓐ Ⓑ ● Ⓓ   3 Ⓐ Ⓑ Ⓒ ●   5 ● Ⓑ Ⓒ Ⓓ   7 Ⓐ Ⓑ Ⓒ ●   9 Ⓐ ● Ⓒ Ⓓ

1

UNIT 1 Vocabulary

Lesson 1: Matching Words with Similar Meanings

Reading Skill: Identifying words that have similar meanings

SAY: **Turn to Lesson 1, Matching Words with Similar Meanings, on page 1.**

Check to see that all students find Lesson 1.

SAY: **In Lesson 1 you will practice matching words that have similar meanings.**

Read the <u>Directions</u> to students.

SAY: **Now look at <u>Try This</u>.**

Read <u>Try This</u> to students.

SAY: **Now look at S1. Read the phrase and the answer choices carefully. Then darken the circle for the word that has the same or almost the same meaning as the word in dark type, *melody*.**

Allow students time to find and mark their answer.

SAY: **Now look at <u>Think It Through</u>.**

Read <u>Think It Through</u> to students. Check to see that all students have filled in the correct answer space. Ask students if they have any questions.

SAY: **Now you will practice matching more words with similar meanings. Do numbers 1 through 9 just as we did S1. When you come to the word *STOP* at the bottom of page 1, put your pencils down. You may now begin.**

Allow students time to find and mark their answers.

Review the questions and answer choices with students. Discuss with the class why one answer is correct and the others are not correct. Also check to see that students have carefully filled in the answer spaces and have completely erased any stray marks.

Unit 1 Test

Unit 1 Test

S1 To feel **drowsy**
- A alert
- B cold
- C confused
- D sleepy

STOP

For questions 1–13, darken the circle for the word or words that mean the same or almost the same as the word in dark type.

1 To pay **homage**
- A honor
- B bearer
- C spite
- D guaranty

2 An interesting **comment**
- J remark
- K image
- L completion
- M story

3 To **simultaneously** link the stations
- A one at a time
- B using lasers
- C with advanced technology
- D at the same time

4 A **meek** office manager
- J easily imposed upon
- K arrogant
- L loud-speaking
- M artistic

5 A **graceful** dancer
- A tall
- B young
- C awkward
- D elegant

6 To **latch** the door
- J beat
- K fasten
- L open
- M paint

7 To **mock** someone's beliefs
- A praise
- B defy
- C ridicule
- D puzzle

8 Require an immediate **response**
- J trial
- K answer
- L reward
- M apology

9 A **stationary** weather front
- A life-threatening
- B unusual
- C not moving
- D approaching

10 To **lodge** a complaint
- J discourage
- K repeat
- L celebrate
- M file

11 To **desire** something
- A claim
- B suspend
- C want
- D repeat

12 To **achieve** a goal
- J go after
- K reach
- L say no to
- M search for

13 Appear **meticulously** groomed
- A sloppily
- B without shoes
- C very carefully
- D out-of-fashion

STOP

Answers

S1 Ⓐ Ⓑ Ⓒ ●	3 Ⓐ Ⓑ Ⓒ ●	6 Ⓙ ● Ⓛ Ⓜ	9 Ⓐ Ⓑ ● Ⓓ	12 Ⓙ ● Ⓛ Ⓜ	Level 11
1 ● Ⓑ Ⓒ Ⓓ	4 ● Ⓚ Ⓛ Ⓜ	7 Ⓐ Ⓑ ● Ⓓ	10 Ⓙ Ⓚ Ⓛ ●	13 Ⓐ Ⓑ ● Ⓓ	
2 ● Ⓚ Ⓛ Ⓜ	5 Ⓐ Ⓑ Ⓒ ●	8 Ⓙ ● Ⓛ Ⓜ	11 Ⓐ Ⓑ ● Ⓓ		

2

SAY: **Turn to the Unit 1 Test on page 2.**

Check to see that all students find the Unit 1 Test.

SAY: **In this test you will use the reading skills that we have practiced in this unit. Now look at S1. Which word has the same or almost the same meaning as the word in dark type? Darken the circle for the correct answer.**

Allow students time to find and mark their answer.

SAY: **You should have darkened the circle for D. Sleepy is closest i meaning to the word in dark type, drowsy.**

Check to see that all students have filled in the correct answer space. As students if they have any questions.

SAY: **Now you will finish the test on your own. Read the directions carefully. Do numbers 1 through 13 just as we did S1. Read t phrases and answer choices carefully. Then darken the circle for each correct answer. When you come to the word STOP a the bottom of page 2, put your pencils down. You may now begin.**

Allow students time to find and mark their answers.

SAY: **It is now time to stop. You have completed the Unit 1 Test. Make sure that you have carefully filled in your answer space and have completely erased any stray marks. Then put your pencils down.**

After the test has been scored, review the questions and answer choices with students. If students are having difficulty with any lesson, provide them with additional practice items.

UNIT 2 Reading Comprehension

Lesson 2: Reading Selections

Directions: Read the story carefully. Darken the circle for the correct answer.

> **TRY THIS** More than one answer choice may seem correct. Choose the answer that goes best with the story.

S1 The story takes place in a far-off land inhabited by humans, elves, hobbits, wizards, and dragons.

This reading selection would probably be found in

A an almanac.

B a fantasy book.

C a biography.

D a science book.

> **THINK IT THROUGH** The correct answer is B. A story with imaginary creatures, such as elves, hobbits, wizards, and dragons, is fiction. It would <u>not</u> be found in an almanac, a biography, or a science book.

STOP

Nature's Cleansing Powder

Snow, an enchanting sight,
Blowing outside, day or night
Slowly, steady
Building on the ground.
Covering the ugliness that winter
Spreads around.
A surly wind blows it into drifts
Much higher than a person's hips.
Then happy children
Make forts, snow dogs, and snowmen—
All kinds of odd forms.
Grumpy people take hours to move it
From one place to another
Only to have the sun come out
And melt it right away.
Leaving behind a dirty, dreary winter day.

1 What does the snow cover?

A Day and night

B Winter's ugliness

C Happy children

D Grumpy people

2 What does the poet mean by "A surly wind blows it into drifts"?

J The snow changes into shapes like snowmen.

K The snow is blown away.

L The snow forms into mounds.

M The snow becomes a blinding blizzard.

3 According to the poet, snow

A is dreaded by young and old alike.

B is an ugly sight day or night.

C always melts as it hits the ground.

D is a beautiful sight.

GO ON

Answers
S1 Ⓐ ● Ⓒ Ⓓ   2 Ⓙ Ⓚ ● Ⓜ
1 Ⓐ ● Ⓒ Ⓓ   3 Ⓐ Ⓑ Ⓒ ●

UNIT 2 Reading Comprehension

Lesson 2: Reading Selections

Reading Skills: Identifying passage details; identifying sequence of events; identifying cause and effect; understanding a character's traits and motives; identifying the main idea; recognizing supporting ideas; identifying theme; predicting outcomes; analyzing author's purpose and effect; understanding vocabulary; identifying genre; making inferences; making generalizations

SAY: **Turn to Lesson 2, Reading Selections, on page 3.**

Check to see that all students find Lesson 2.

SAY: **In Lesson 2 you will practice answering questions about selections that you read.**

Read the <u>Directions</u> to students.

SAY: **Now look at <u>Try This</u>.**

Read <u>Try This</u> to students.

SAY: **Now look at S1. Read the selection silently. Then choose the answer that correctly completes the sentence. Darken the circle for the correct answer.**

Allow students time to find and mark their answer.

SAY: **Now look at <u>Think It Through</u>.**

Read <u>Think It Through</u> to students. Check to see that all students have filled in the correct answer space. Ask students if they have any questions.

SAY: **Now you will practice answering more questions about selections that you read. Beginning on page 3, read each selection carefully and answer the questions that follow. Do numbers 1 through 19 just as we did S1. When you come to the words *GO ON* at the bottom of a page, continue working on the next page. When you come to the word *STOP* at the bottom of page 7, put your pencils down. You may now begin.**

Allow students time to find and mark their answers.

"I can't believe that you and I are both finalists in the Amazon Rain Forest Adventure!" shouted Jess to her friend and fellow environmentalist.

"It is highly unusual for the government to choose two students from the same school for this educational journey. But we both worked hard on our science experiments, and our essays about why we wanted to go on this trip were chosen first and second in the state. Also, Mr. Hancock recommended both of us to the selection committee," Winnie responded with enthusiasm.

Jess and Winnie were both members of the school's Environmental Impact Committee (EIC). They constructed posters explaining the importance of the rain forests and how they provide the earth with forty percent of its oxygen supply by converting carbon dioxide into oxygen. Jess and Winnie also contacted speakers from the Environmental Protection Agency (EPA). These speakers conducted a school assembly showing the kinds of animals and plants that live in the rain forests and are in danger of becoming extinct as the rain forests disappear.

The girls' two-week trip to Brazil's Amazon Rain Forest started in Macapá, a city located at the mouth of the Amazon River. There were eight other students in their group. Four adults guided the students on a six-hour canoe trip down the Amazon. Along their journey they saw piranha (fish with razor-sharp teeth), alligators, monkeys, passion-fruit trees, and outstanding flowers in every color imaginable. When the group reached Manaus they made themselves comfortable in a cabin near the river.

"The first night in the cabin was the most unforgettable experience. All night long I could hear the cries of wild animals, but of course I could see nothing because there were no lights near our cabin. I was nervous and afraid to sleep," said Winnie in a presentation to fellow students upon returning home from Brazil.

"I was so tired that first night from canoeing for six hours that I slept very well," explained Jess.

"I was impressed with the difficult life of the people who live in the rain forest. They have none of the conveniences that we take for granted. They love their environment, though, and do not abuse it. I think this is partly because they are very dependent on their environment for the things they need to live," said Winnie.

"While I was in the rain forest enjoying its beauty and unique ecosystem, I thought about what I could do to help save the rain forest," said Jess. "I've decided to design a reusable container for use in grocery stores instead of grocery bags. This will lessen the number of trees cut down to make the bags. I hope to sell the bags to consumers and use the profits to buy and preserve as many acres of rain forest as possible," explained Jess.

GO ON

Level 11

4

4 The best title for this selection might be

   J "Science Experiments"

   K "Contest Winners"

   L "Amazon Rain Forest Adventure"

   M "The History of Rain Forests"

5 What is the main topic of the second paragraph?

   A The selection of school assembly ideas

   B Why Jess and Winnie were chosen for a trip to the rain forest of Brazil

   C How Jess and Winnie became interested in environmental causes

   D The people who lived in the rain forest

6 What is the meaning of the word "extinct" in the third paragraph?

   J No longer existing

   K No longer active

   L No longer burning

   M No longer being used

7 The description of the girls' journey down the Amazon River in the fourth paragraph helps the reader to understand

   A the work done by the Environmental Protection Agency.

   B the environment of a rain forest.

   C the enthusiasm the girls felt for their trip.

   D the rain forest at night.

8 What word best describes Jess and Winnie?

   J Secretive   **L** Foolish

   K Cowardly   **M** Concerned

9 Winnie explained why she was afraid the first night in the cabin so that

   A her fellow students would understand how she felt.

   B Jess would admit that she too was afraid at night.

   C people listening to her story would know why she did not like her trip.

   D her friends would be afraid to visit the rain forest.

10 How does Winnie feel about the people of the rain forest?

   J She fears them.

   K She feels sorry for them because they are dependent on the rain forest for their needs.

   L She feels angry with them for the way they misuse the rain forest.

   M She admires them for the way in which they treat their environment.

11 What has Jess decided to do to help save the rain forest?

   A She wants to go back to Brazil and live in the rain forest.

   B She wants to protest the destruction of the rain forest at the house of the ambassador from Brazil.

   C She wants to become a worker at the Environmental Protection Agency.

   D She wants to design grocery bags to help reduce the number of trees cut down to make bags.

GO ON

Answers

4 Ⓙ Ⓚ ● Ⓜ   6 ● Ⓚ Ⓛ Ⓜ   8 Ⓙ Ⓚ Ⓛ ●   10 Ⓙ Ⓚ Ⓛ ●

5 Ⓐ ● Ⓒ Ⓓ   7 Ⓐ ● Ⓒ Ⓓ   9 ● Ⓑ Ⓒ Ⓓ   11 Ⓐ Ⓑ Ⓒ ●

5

The February wind blew chill across the prairie. Mae and Milly huddled together in the wagon, trying to stay warm. Soon their father would stop to make camp for the night. Then they could build a fire to warm themselves. The sisters watched their mother. She was swaying with the motion of the wagon as she mended their clothes. When they reached their new home on the frontier, there would be no store nearby to buy new things. They would have to make do with what they had. That seemed both scary and exciting to the girls. This move was really an adventure.

Suddenly the girls heard their father shout, "Quick! Come up here and look at this!" The girls and their mother crawled to the front of the wagon, opened the flap, and looked out upon a large herd of buffalo. The powerful animals with their brown shaggy coats moved slowly toward the south. They kept their backs to the wind, which seemed to blow colder as the day progressed.

"This might be a good stopping place. It looks like we might be in for some bad weather," said Father. Clouds were gathering on the northern horizon as the family prepared for the night. Mae helped her father look for dry brush to start a fire, while Milly and her mother made preparations for dinner. They all worked quickly, sensing that they had a long, hard night ahead.

12 According to the story, how many family members are making the journey?

J Three

K Four

L Five

M Seven

13 This story most likely was written to

A describe how to mend clothes.

B tell about a family's journey west.

C teach the reader how to make camp.

D describe how buffalo cross the prairie.

14 The family was traveling in

J a canoe.

K a railroad compartment.

L a covered wagon.

M a houseboat.

15 Why was the family expecting a long, hard night?

A Because of trouble with the buffalo

B Because the weather was threatening to turn bad

C Because their food was lost on the journey

D Because they had lost direction in a windstorm.

GO ON

Answers

6

12 Ⓙ ● Ⓛ Ⓜ   14 Ⓙ Ⓚ ● Ⓜ

13 Ⓐ ● Ⓒ Ⓓ   15 Ⓐ ● Ⓒ Ⓓ

People have been making pottery since prehistoric times. Early pottery consisted of simple household utensils such as bowls and storage jars.

Pottery is made from clay. The clay is shaped and put into a special oven called a kiln. The pottery is then fired, or baked, at a very high temperature, until it hardens. Sometimes a glaze is applied so the pottery can hold water or other liquids.

Our prehistoric ancestors began making pottery about 11,000 B.C. In about 3000 B.C., the Egyptians became the first people to glaze their pottery. People in China, North and South America, and Africa were all making pottery around this time. Originally, pottery was shaped by hand. The potter rolled out coils of clay and stacked the coils one atop another. Another method was simply to pinch the clay into the desired shape. But in China, about 1500 B.C., potters started to use a potter's wheel. The wheel enabled the potter to work faster than shaping the clay by hand. The potter kicked a bottom wheel with the foot while shaping the clay by hand on the upper wheel.

Today most potter's wheels are electric. Modern potters use both the wheel and the older hand-shaping methods to create art objects, as well as the household utensils that potters have been making for thousands of years.

16 **How long have people been making pottery?**

J   One hundred years

K   One thousand years

L   Nineteen hundred and ninety years

M   Many thousands of years

17 **This selection is mostly about**

A   how pottery is glazed.

B   how the potter's wheel was invented.

C   the history of pottery.

D   how to make clay.

18 **Why did prehistoric people make objects out of clay?**

J   They wanted to bring beauty into their lives.

K   It was a good way to pass the time.

L   They needed bowls and storage jars.

M   Pottery making was important in their religion.

19 **What makes the clay harden?**

A   It is frozen.

B   It is fired.

C   It is molded in lava.

D   It is spun on a wheel.

STOP

Answers
16 Ⓙ Ⓚ Ⓛ ●   18 Ⓙ Ⓚ ● Ⓜ
17 Ⓐ Ⓑ ● Ⓓ   19 Ⓐ ● Ⓒ Ⓓ

S1 Jake looks forward to spring because he plays baseball. During fall and winter, however he has to sell calendars to raise funds. The money from calendar sales pays for his team uniform.

What does Jake do before baseball season begins?

A He practices at the batting cage.

B He sells calendars to raise funds.

C He gets fitted for a uniform.

D He jogs to get in shape.

STOP

For questions 1–18, darken the circle for the correct answer.

In some parts of the world, food shortages cause many people to starve. Somehow, the world's food crop (the amount of food being produced in the world) must be increased. In order to help this happen, scientists have begun to study little-known, edible plants. There are about 20,000 kinds of edible plants, although only about a hundred of them are grown as food crops.

Amaranth and leucaena are two plants that have the potential for becoming useful food crops in the near future. Amaranth is a grain that has been eaten in Mexico for hundreds of years. It can grow in a variety of climates and soils, has many uses and is rich in nutrients. Amaranth tastes good and can be ground and used as flour or popped like corn. Leucaena is a fast-growing tree that may become a popular food source of the future. This tall tree grows very fast. It can also be used for making fuel.

As time goes on, more plants are being discovered and rediscovered. Scientists hope that these plants will help solve the world's food crisis.

1 The selection is mainly about

A eating vegetables instead of meat.

B the use of little-known plants to solve the world's food problems.

C food shortages in Africa.

D methods of growing plants.

2 From the selection, you can conclude that

J meat will not be available in the future.

K there are probably many edible plants that we haven't discovered.

L leucaena is just like broccoli.

M amaranth will be used most in the future.

3 About how many edible plants are there?

A 100

B 20,000

C 2

D 20

4 What is stated in the selection as an advantage of the amaranth plant?

J It is better than leucaena.

K The tree grows fast and is very tall.

L It can grow in many climates and soils.

M It can also be used to solve the world's fuel problems.

GO ON

Level 11

Answers

S1 Ⓐ ● Ⓒ Ⓓ   2 Ⓙ ● Ⓛ Ⓜ   4 Ⓙ Ⓚ ● Ⓜ

8   1 Ⓐ ● Ⓒ Ⓓ   3 Ⓐ ● Ⓒ Ⓓ

Unit 2 Test

SAY: **Turn to the Unit 2 Test on page 8.**

Check to see that all students find the Unit 2 Test.

SAY: **In this test you will use the reading skills that we have practiced in this unit. Look at S1. Read the selection silently. Then answer the question that follows. What does Jake do before baseball season begins? Darken the circle for the correct answer.**

Allow students time to find and mark their answers.

SAY: **You should have darkened the circle for *B* because the selection states that during the fall and winter Jake sells calendars to raise funds that pay for his team uniform.**

Check to see that all students have filled in the correct answer space. As students if they have any questions.

SAY: **Now you will finish the test on your own. Read the directions for each selection. Then carefully read each selection and the questions that follow. Do numbers 1 through 18 just as we did S1. Darken the circle for each correct answer. When you come to the words *GO ON* at the bottom of a page, continue working on the next page. When you come to the word *STOP* at the bottom of page 11, put your pencils down. You may now begin.**

Allow students time to find and mark their answers.

In this story, Dawn and her brother Greg, help clean their grandmother's flooded home.

The newspaper headlines claimed that the flood was a once-in-a-lifetime event. People in the soggy farm town in Iowa certainly hoped that was true. The Mississippi River knew no banks for two weeks in August. The mess that the flood left behind would take an incredible amount of time, money, and energy to clean.

When Dawn and Greg arrived on the bus at their grandmother's farm town, they didn't recognize much. They saw a lot of debris including parts of homes, pieces of furniture, piles of sandbags, and acres of slimy mud. Here and there they could even see dead fish that had been left behind when the waters receded.

Grandmother was anxious to greet Dawn and Greg and get back to the house to start their daunting clean-up chores. Her car had been ruined in the flood so they walked the mile to the house.

"Grandma, how badly damaged was your house?" asked Dawn as they slopped through the mud.

"Well, the house is still standing but it is covered with the same kind of slimy mud we're walking in," replied Grandma.

"You mean this mud came through the doors and windows?" asked Greg incredulously.

"I'm afraid the force of the water and mud broke the basement windows and filled the house up to the second story with river water, silt, and fish," said Grandma sadly.

5 **Why didn't Dawn and Greg recognize their grandmother's town?**

A They had never been there before.

B They hadn't visited there in many years.

C The flood had severely damaged the town.

D The town had been remodeled after the flood.

6 **What does the word "receded" mean in the second paragraph?**

J Advanced

K Rose

L Disproved

M Withdrew

7 **Why did Grandma, Dawn, and Greg walk the mile to Grandma's house?**

A Grandma's car had been ruined in the flood.

B The roads were ruined and impassable as a result of the floods.

C Dawn and Greg needed some exercise after their long bus ride.

D They wanted to walk in order to see the damage left behind by the river.

8 **In the sixth paragraph, Greg's reaction to his grandmother's explanation of the damage to her house shows the reader that**

J Greg wasn't surprised.

K Greg couldn't believe what his grandmother told him.

L Greg wasn't listening to his grandmother.

M Greg couldn't hear what his grandmother was saying.

GO ON

Answers
5 Ⓐ Ⓑ Ⓒ Ⓓ   7 Ⓐ Ⓑ Ⓒ Ⓓ
6 Ⓙ Ⓚ Ⓛ Ⓜ   8 Ⓙ Ⓚ Ⓛ Ⓜ

Matt and his big brother Jesse were walking along the beach. Jesse was home from college for the summer. The boys had time on their hands. As they walked, Matt picked up an oyster shell.

"This reminds me of those great smoked oysters Dad made last fall," said Matt.

"You always have loved oysters," laughed Jesse. "Let me tell you what I learned about oysters this year."

Jesse picked up an oyster shell and rolled it over in his hand. "Did you know that baby oysters do not have shells? They are little, round creatures, about the size of a head of a pin. They swim around by moving tiny hairs on their bodies. When an oyster is one day old, it starts to form a hard shell. In about a week, the shell is fully formed. That is when the oyster finds a rock to attach itself to. It stays there for the rest of its life.

"The oyster shell is really two shells. They are held together by a hinge that is part of the oyster's body. When the lid of the shell is open, the oyster is in danger. You see, you are not the only one that likes to eat them. Many sea animals love oysters, too.

"The oyster has no eyes or ears. Tiny feelers tell the oyster when it is in danger. When this happens, the shell lid slams shut, keeping the oyster safe inside. Many hungry fish, seals, and otters have been turned away by a tightly shut oyster shell."

"You do know a lot about oysters," said Matt. "What else did you learn?"

"Well," said Jesse, "oysters are members of a family called mollusks. Mollusks all have soft bodies without bones. Clams and snails are also members of this family. Other mollusks like octopuses and slugs do not have shells."

"Jesse, I hate to cut this walk short," said Matt. "All your talk about oysters is making me hungry. Let's head home for lunch."

9 In the first paragraph, what does the phrase "had time on their hands" mean?

A Had extra time

B Had to watch the time

C Had to hurry

D Had to wash their hands

10 Which statement about baby oysters is not true?

J They are small and round.

K They are surrounded by a soft shell.

L They swim by moving tiny hairs.

M They are about the size of a head of a pin.

11 About how long does it take for an oyster shell to fully form?

A One hour

B One day

C One week

D One year

12 Which of these events was happening as the story took place?

J Jesse arrived home from college.

K Matt ate smoked oysters.

L Matt and Jesse walked along the beach.

M Matt and Jesse went fishing.

GO ON

Level 11

Answers
9 Ⓐ Ⓑ Ⓒ Ⓓ   11 Ⓐ Ⓑ Ⓒ Ⓓ
10   10 Ⓙ Ⓚ Ⓛ Ⓜ   12 Ⓙ Ⓚ Ⓛ Ⓜ

Once there was a terrible fire in a forest. The only way for a group of monkeys to survive was to escape into a river. The river had a fast current that swept the monkeys downstream. After several minutes all the monkeys were able to grab hold of a large branch. They floated on the branch for hours. The monkeys fell asleep from exhaustion. When they awoke, they found themselves marooned on the shore of an island.

The monkeys investigated the island and found that there were plenty of trees and generous amounts of food to eat. All the monkeys came to accept their new home, except one named Reggie. Reggie missed his old environment. He wanted to go back, but there was no way to do that.

As time passed, Reggie became lazy. He spent his days napping in the shade. The other monkeys tried to get Reggie to play with them.

"Reggie, come swing in the trees with us. Exercise, you'll feel better," they would shout to Reggie.

"Why should I? Life is uninteresting. Especially being stranded on this island. Just leave me alone. I'm tired. I'm also young. I have the rest of my life to do those kinds of things. Maybe I'll feel like doing that tomorrow," would be his reply.

One day while Reggie was napping, a trapper came to the island to capture animals for his small zoo in a nearby country. The other monkeys saw the trapper and warned Reggie. Reggie got up to run away, but he had grown fat and slow. The trapper easily imprisoned Reggie in a net. The other monkeys were strong and healthy and had no problem running away and climbing trees to escape capture.

13 According to the selection, which of these events happened last?

A The monkeys were in a forest fire.

B The monkeys were stranded on an island.

C Reggie was captured by an animal trapper.

D Reggie napped in the shade.

14 In this selection, the word "marooned" means

J stopped.

K colored red.

L released.

M stranded.

15 Which of these proverbs best fit this selection?

A If at first you don't succeed, try, try again.

B A penny saved is a penny earned.

C Enjoy life as it is today, tomorrow may never come.

D A stitch in time saves nine.

16 This story most likely would be found in a book of

J fables.

K facts.

L biographies.

M myths.

STOP

Level 11

Answers
13 Ⓐ Ⓑ Ⓒ Ⓓ   15 Ⓐ Ⓑ Ⓒ Ⓓ
14 Ⓙ Ⓚ Ⓛ Ⓜ   16 Ⓙ Ⓚ Ⓛ Ⓜ

11

SAY: **It is now time to stop. You have completed the Unit 2 Test. Make sure that you have carefully filled in your answer spaces and have completely erased any stray marks. Then put your pencils down.**

After the test has been scored, review the questions and answer choices with students. If students are having difficulty, provide them with additional practice.

Lesson 3: Checking Word Spellings

Directions: Darken the circle for the word that is <u>not</u> spelled correctly. Darken the circle for *No mistakes* if all the words are spelled correctly.

> **TRY THIS**   First, decide which words you know are spelled correctly. Then, look at the remaining words to make your choice. Be sure to look at all the words.

S1 A trench
    B releef
    C obtain
    D title
    E (No mistakes)

> **THINK IT THROUGH**   The correct answer is B. The word releef is spelled incorrectly. The correct spelling is r-e-l-i-e-f. Notice that an e comes after the l in the answer choice. The other choices are spelled correctly.

STOP

1 A stung B award C territory D underneath E (No mistakes)	4 J aluminum K achievement L apeal M autograph N (No mistakes)	7 A explosion B sience C fertile D rhythm E (No mistakes)
2 J peacefull K universe L balcony M opinion N (No mistakes)	5 A painted B chanel C disaster D emergency E (No mistakes)	8 J ambitious K gravul L genuine M rink N (No mistakes)
3 A spinach B opposite C symbol D colonie E (No mistakes)	6 J absorb K stitch L blunder M demonstrait N (No mistakes)	9 A restaurant B embroider C border D festival E (No mistakes)

STOP

Level 11

UNIT 3 Spelling

Lesson 3: Checking Word Spellings

Language Skill: Identifying correct spellings of words; recognizing misspelled words

SAY: **Turn to Lesson 3, Checking Word Spellings, on page 12.**

Check to see that all students find Lesson 3.

SAY: **In Lesson 3 you will practice checking the spelling of words.**

Read the <u>Directions</u> to students.

SAY: **Now look at <u>Try This</u>.**

Read <u>Try This</u> to students.

SAY: **Now look at S1. Read the answer choices carefully. Then darken the circle for the word that is not spelled correctly. Darken the circle for *No mistakes* if all the words are spelled correctly.**

Allow students time to find and mark their answer.

SAY: **Now look at <u>Think It Through</u>.**

Read <u>Think It Through</u> to students. Check to see that all students have filled in the correct answer space. Ask students if they have any question

SAY: **Now you will practice checking the spelling for more words. I numbers 1 through 9 just as we did S1. When you come to the word *STOP* at the bottom of page 12, put your pencils down. You may now begin.**

Allow students time to find and mark their answers.

Review the questions and answer choices with students. Discuss with th class why one answer is correct and the others are not correct. Also che to see that students have carefully filled in the answer spaces and have completely erased any stray marks.

S1
A witnes
B admission
C horizon
D gasoline
E (No mistakes)

STOP

For questions 1–16, darken the circle for the word that is not spelled correctly. Darken the circle for *No mistakes* if all the words are spelled correctly.

1
A immediate
B presecute
C outwit
D scramble
E (No mistakes)

2
J frost
K saplings
L esels
M celebrations
N (No mistakes)

3
A university
B hike
C irrigate
D erace
E (No mistakes)

4
J quaranteen
K possession
L solid
M tablet
N (No mistakes)

5
A spoubt
B visible
C elections
D appreciate
E (No mistakes)

6
J globe
K dresser
L stubborn
M capitol
N (No mistakes)

7
A advize
B community
C furnished
D bolder
E (No mistakes)

8
J ankle
K choir
L fountain
M voluntear
N (No mistakes)

9
A automatic
B imagenary
C drought
D poisonous
E (No mistakes)

10
J population
K chemistry
L fleet
M doornob
N (No mistakes)

11
A dissolve
B displease
C dispute
D dispoze
E (No mistakes)

12
J gymnasium
K desend
L invitation
M correction
N (No mistakes)

13
A tissue
B nazal
C weird
D cartridge
E (No mistakes)

14
J rummage
K vacant
L agreement
M decreace
N (No mistakes)

15
A cazually
B pain
C tusk
D foster
E (No mistakes)

16
J hight
K knelt
L lingered
M argued
N (No mistakes)

STOP

Answers
S1 ● Ⓑ Ⓒ Ⓓ Ⓔ
1 Ⓐ ● Ⓒ Ⓓ Ⓔ
2 Ⓙ ● Ⓛ Ⓜ Ⓝ
3 Ⓐ Ⓑ Ⓒ ● Ⓔ
4 ● Ⓚ Ⓛ Ⓜ Ⓝ
5 ● Ⓑ Ⓒ Ⓓ Ⓔ
6 Ⓙ Ⓚ Ⓛ ● Ⓝ
7 ● Ⓑ Ⓒ Ⓓ Ⓔ
8 Ⓙ Ⓚ Ⓛ ● Ⓝ
9 Ⓐ ● Ⓒ Ⓓ Ⓔ
10 Ⓙ Ⓚ Ⓛ ● Ⓝ
11 Ⓐ Ⓑ Ⓒ ● Ⓔ
12 Ⓙ ● Ⓛ Ⓜ Ⓝ
13 Ⓐ ● Ⓒ Ⓓ Ⓔ
14 Ⓙ Ⓚ Ⓛ ● Ⓝ
15 ● Ⓑ Ⓒ Ⓓ Ⓔ
16 ● Ⓚ Ⓛ Ⓜ Ⓝ

Level 11

13

Unit 3 Test

SAY: **Turn to the Unit 3 Test on page 13.**

Check to see that all students find the Unit 3 Test.

SAY: **In this test you will use the language skills that we have practiced in this unit. We will work the sample exercise together before you begin the test. Look at S1. Read the answer choices carefully. Then darken the circle for the word that is not spelled correctly. Darken the circle for *No mistakes* if all the words are spelled correctly.**

Allow students time to find and mark their answer.

SAY: **You should have darkened the circle for *A* because it shows an incorrect spelling for the word *witness*.**

Check to see that all students have filled in the correct answer space. Ask students if they have any questions.

SAY: **Now you will finish the test on your own. Read the directions carefully. Do numbers 1 through 16 just as we did the sample. Read the answer choices carefully. Then darken the circle for each correct answer. When you come to the word *STOP* at the bottom of page 13, put your pencils down. You may now begin.**

Allow students time to find and mark their answers.

SAY: **It is now time to stop. You have completed the Unit 3 Test. Make sure that you have carefully filled in your answer spaces and have completely erased any stray marks. Then put your pencils down.**

After the test has been scored, review the questions and answer choices with students. If students are having difficulty with any lesson, provide them with additional practice items.

UNIT 4 Language Mechanics

Lesson 4: Using Correct Capitalization

Directions: Darken the circle for the line that has a capitalization error. Darken the circle for *No mistakes* if there is no capitalization error.

> **TRY THIS**
>
> First, read the entire sentence. Then look at each line for a word that should be capitalized or a word that should not be capitalized.

S1 A The name of my Dentist is
    B Dr. Summer, but she
    C prefers to be called Dr. Shari.
    D *(No mistakes)*

> **THINK IT THROUGH**
>
> The correct answer is A. Dentist should not be capitalized, since it is a common noun. Lines B and C do not contain any errors.

STOP

---

1 A The parade will begin tomorrow
   B morning at the corner of
   C Center street and Sixth Avenue.
   D *(No mistakes)*

5 A Millions of people from all over
   B the world travel to Orlando,
   C florida, to visit Disney World.
   D *(No mistakes)*

2 J As soon as the days get
   K warmer, Taylor park will be
   L filled with young children.
   M *(No mistakes)*

6 J Many Native American groups
   K once hunted buffalo on the Great
   L Plains of the United States.
   M *(No mistakes)*

3 A Nowadays people of every age
   B wear sneakers. In fact, even my
   C Grandma has a pair of them.
   D *(No mistakes)*

7 A "Could you help me look for my
   B blue shirt?" asked Jenny. "i can't
   C find it anywhere in my room."
   D *(No mistakes)*

4 J Lynn and roland rode the train
   K through the park on Saturday.
   L They can't wait to go again!
   M *(No mistakes)*

8 J The company that publishes
   K *National Geographic* publishes
   L *world*, a magazine for children.
   M *(No mistakes)*

GO ON

Level 11

Answers
S1 ● Ⓑ Ⓒ Ⓓ   2 Ⓙ ● Ⓛ Ⓜ   4 ● Ⓚ Ⓛ Ⓜ   6 Ⓙ Ⓚ Ⓛ ●   8 Ⓙ Ⓚ ● Ⓜ
14 1 Ⓐ Ⓑ ● Ⓓ   3 Ⓐ Ⓑ ● Ⓓ   5 Ⓐ Ⓑ ● Ⓓ   7 Ⓐ ● Ⓒ Ⓓ

UNIT 4 Language Mechanics

Lesson 4: Using Correct Capitalization

Language Skill: Identifying the need for capitalization in sentences

SAY: **Turn to Lesson 4, Using Correct Capitalization, on page 14.**

Check to see that all students find Lesson 4.

SAY: **In Lesson 4 you will practice finding capitalization errors in sentences.**

Read the <u>Directions</u> to students.

SAY: **Now look at <u>Try This</u>.**

Read <u>Try This</u> to students.

SAY: **Now look at S1. Read the lines silently. Then darken the circle for the line that shows a mistake in capitalization. Darken the circle for *No mistakes* if there is no capitalization error.**

Allow students time to find and mark their answer.

SAY: **Now look at <u>Think It Through</u>.**

Read <u>Think It Through</u> to students. Check to see that all students have filled in the correct answer space. Ask students if they have any questions.

SAY: **Now you will practice finding capitalization errors in more sentences. Do numbers 1 through 22 just as we did S1. When you come to the words *GO ON* at the bottom of page 14, continue working on the next page. When you come to the word *STOP* at the bottom of page 15, put your pencils down. You may now begin.**

Allow students time to find and mark their answers.

Review the questions and answer choices with students. Discuss with the class why one answer is correct and the others are not correct. Also check to see that students have carefully filled in the answer spaces and have completely erased any stray marks.

9 A When my aunt was nine years
   B old, she wrote every month
   C to her pen pal in england.
   D *(No mistakes)*

10 J   570 Masonic ave.
    K   San Jose, CA 95707
    L   March 12, 1995
    M *(No mistakes)*

11 A Pet Paws Pet shop
    B San Francisco, CA 95319
    C Dear Manager:
    D *(No mistakes)*

12 J Do you carry the book *caring*
    K *for Tropical Fish*? I need help
    L with my new aquarium.
    M *(No mistakes)*

13 A I appreciate your help.
    B   Sincerely yours,
    C   Freddie Munoz
    D *(No mistakes)*

14 J My neighbor, colonel James A.
    K McGuire, has served in the
    L Marines since he was nineteen.
    M *(No mistakes)*

15 A The American Heart Association
    B suggests low-fat foods
    C and exercise to stay healthy.
    D *(No mistakes)*

16 J My cousins Mercy and Manuel
    K will name their new kitten cali
    L because it has calico markings.
    M *(No mistakes)*

17 A Have you ever been swimming
    B in the Medina river? It's one of
    C my favorite places in Texas.
    D *(No mistakes)*

18 J If Miko leaves on Monday, she
    K should get to our house in Salt
    L Lake City by Tuesday Evening.
    M *(No mistakes)*

19 A Before we went to Quebec,
    B we studied french so we
    C could understand the language.
    D *(No mistakes)*

20 J Every Wednesday I go to my
    K martial arts class. someday, I
    L hope to get my black belt.
    M *(No mistakes)*

21 A Many well-known artists,
    B such as Botticelli and
    C picasso, were born in Europe.
    D *(No mistakes)*

22 J Spanish people lived in
    K New mexico for centuries
    L before white settlers arrived.
    M *(No mistakes)*

STOP

Answers

9 ⒶⒷ●Ⓓ	12 ●ⓀⓁⓂ	15 ⒶⒷⒸ●	18 ⒿⓀ●Ⓜ	21 ⒶⒷ●Ⓓ	Level 11
10 ●ⓀⓁⓂ	13 ⒶⒷⒸ●	16 Ⓙ●ⓁⓂ	19 Ⓐ●ⒸⒹ	22 Ⓙ●ⓁⓂ	
11 ●ⒷⒸⒹ	14 ●ⓀⓁⓂ	17 Ⓐ●ⒸⒹ	20 Ⓙ●ⓁⓂ		**15**

Lesson 5: Using Correct Punctuation

Directions: Darken the circle for the line that has a punctuation error. Darken the circle for *No mistakes* if there is no punctuation error.

> **TRY THIS** Read the sentence carefully. Then check each line closely. Think about where you would put the punctuation marks if you were writing the sentence.

S1
A Do you think these bright
B green laces match my
C blue and white sneakers
D *(No mistakes)*

> **THINK IT THROUGH** The correct answer is C. All sentences should end with a punctuation mark. Line C has a punctuation error because it should end with a question mark.

STOP

1
A Every day at 1200 noon,
B the loud factory whistle
C is heard all over town.
D *(No mistakes)*

2
J Since I have not done my
K chores today, I will have to
L do double work tomorrow.
M *(No mistakes)*

3
A Christopher needs new pants,
B shirts sweaters and a coat
C since he has grown four inches.
D *(No mistakes)*

4
J I don't want Jill to come with
K us to the movies. Shes always
L scared and wants to go home.
M *(No mistakes)*

5
A The city of Cranston, Utah,
B was named for its founder,
C TW Maxwell Cranston.
D *(No mistakes)*

6
J "Can you help me work out
K the answer to this math
L problem? asked Susannah.
M *(No mistakes)*

7
A On November 16 1988
B three-year-old Rusty saw
C his first Walt Disney movie.
D *(No mistakes)*

8
J We planted cucumbers, and
K tomatoes in our garden this
L spring. I can't wait to eat them!
M *(No mistakes)*

GO ON

Level 11

Answers

16

S1 Ⓐ Ⓑ ● Ⓓ   2 Ⓙ Ⓚ Ⓛ ●   4 Ⓙ ● Ⓛ Ⓜ   6 Ⓙ Ⓚ ● Ⓜ   8 ● Ⓚ Ⓛ Ⓜ
1 ● Ⓑ Ⓒ Ⓓ   3 Ⓐ ● Ⓒ Ⓓ   5 Ⓐ Ⓑ ● Ⓓ   7 ● Ⓑ Ⓒ Ⓓ

Lesson 5: Using Correct Punctuation

Language Skill: Identifying the need for punctuation in sentences

SAY: **Turn to Lesson 5, Using Correct Punctuation, on page 16.**

Check to see that all students find Lesson 5.

SAY: **In Lesson 5 you will practice finding punctuation errors in sentences.**

Read the <u>Directions</u> to students.

SAY: **Now look at <u>Try This</u>.**

Read <u>Try This</u> to students.

SAY: **Now look at S1. Read the lines silently. Then darken the circle for the line that has a punctuation error. Darken the circle for *No mistakes* if there is no punctuation error.**

Allow students time to find and mark their answer.

SAY: **Now look at <u>Think It Through</u>.**

Read <u>Think It Through</u> to students. Check to see that all students have filled in the correct answer space. Ask students if they have any questions.

SAY: **Now you will practice finding punctuation errors in more sentences. Do numbers 1 through 22 just as we did S1. When you come to the words *GO ON* at the bottom of page 16, continue working on the next page. When you come to the word *STOP* at the bottom of page 17, put your pencils down. You may now begin.**

Allow students time to find and mark their answers.

9   A   Why does it rain so much in May
    B   Flowers need water, but our
    C   baseball games get rained out.
    D   *(No mistakes)*

10   J   My aunt and uncle are going to
    K   San Francisco, California for
    L   their vacation this summer.
    M   *(No mistakes)*

11   A   Arizona's Grand Canyon is just
    B   breathtaking! Can you believe
    C   it's really a natural wonder?
    D   *(No mistakes)*

12   J   Maria said, "I just read a
    K   great story about a dog's
    L   adventures on a spaceship."
    M   *(No mistakes)*

13   A   Didnt I see your picture
    B   on page twelve of the local
    C   newspaper last Thursday?
    D   *(No mistakes)*

14   J   I really enjoy watching the birds
    K   that come to our feeder We
    L   get finches, jays, and sparrows.
    M   *(No mistakes)*

15   A   Cynthia takes special care of
    B   her cat's. She brushes them
    C   and plays with them every day.
    D   *(No mistakes)*

16   J   19 Sparrow Hawk Rd.
    K   Mesa AZ 86036
    L   May 19, 1995
    M   *(No mistakes)*

17   A   U S Senator's Office
    B   Phoenix, AZ 86021
    C   Dear Senator:
    D   *(No mistakes)*

18   J   My grandfather's hundredth
    K   birthday is next week. Could you
    L   send him a birthday card?
    M   *(No mistakes)*

19   A   He is one of your biggest fans.
    B   Sincerely yours,
    C   Nathan Klatt
    D   *(No mistakes)*

20   J   Does Lee want to go swimming
    K   with us?" asked Dolores, "or
    L   does he have to go home early?"
    M   *(No mistakes)*

21   A   In 1789, our Constitution, was
    B   adopted. Have you ever
    C   heard of the Bill of Rights?
    D   *(No mistakes)*

22   J   My favorite kind of pizza
    K   has extra cheese pepperoni,
    L   meatballs, and mushrooms.
    M   *(No mistakes)*

STOP

Answers

9 ● Ⓑ Ⓒ Ⓓ   12 Ⓙ Ⓚ Ⓛ ●   15 Ⓐ ● Ⓒ Ⓓ   18 Ⓙ Ⓚ Ⓛ ●   21 ● Ⓑ Ⓒ Ⓓ   Level 11
10 Ⓙ ● Ⓛ Ⓜ   13 ● Ⓑ Ⓒ Ⓓ   16 Ⓙ ● Ⓛ Ⓜ   19 Ⓐ Ⓑ Ⓒ ●   22 Ⓙ ● Ⓛ Ⓜ
11 Ⓐ Ⓑ Ⓒ ●   14 Ⓙ ● Ⓛ Ⓜ   17 ● Ⓑ Ⓒ Ⓓ   20 ● Ⓚ Ⓛ Ⓜ   **17**

S1
A Last year uncle Toby became
B a math professor at George
C Mason University in Virginia.
D (No mistakes)

STOP

S2
J Dr. Ellen M Green traveled
K to the Middle East to study
L languages and customs.
M (No mistakes)

STOP

For questions 1–11, darken the circle for the line that has a capitalization error. Darken the circle for *No mistakes* if there is no capitalization error.

1
A Earth as we know it will not
B last unless we take care of it.
C we can help by not littering.
D (No mistakes)

2
J Ana and Linda like to go to
K Stinson beach every Saturday
L morning during the summer.
M (No mistakes)

3
A Did you see or hear about
B the three-alarm fire in the
C apartments on lee Terrace?
D (No mistakes)

4
J The English Channel is a
K large body of water that lies
L between England and France.
M (No mistakes)

5
A Because we live less than a
B mile away, my brother and I
C cannot take the bus to School.
D (No mistakes)

6
J The Red cross organization
K tries to help people around the
L world who are sick or suffering.
M (No mistakes)

7
A We have a new student in class.
B He was born in the andes
C Mountains in South America.
D (No mistakes)

8
J To get to Jason's Deli, walk to
K Main Street. Turn right, and
L then right again on Oak street.
M (No mistakes)

9
A In August, Ling will
B visit her grandparents
C who live in Taiwan.
D (No mistakes)

10
J *Green Eggs and Ham* is the
K best of all the many
L books that dr. Seuss wrote.
M (No mistakes)

11
A We wear red, white, and blue,
B and we display the American
C flag on the fourth of July.
D (No mistakes)

GO ON

Answers
S1 ● Ⓑ Ⓒ Ⓓ   2 Ⓙ ● Ⓛ Ⓜ   5 Ⓐ Ⓑ ● Ⓓ   8 Ⓙ Ⓚ ● Ⓜ   11 Ⓐ Ⓑ ● Ⓓ   Level 11
S2 ● Ⓚ Ⓛ Ⓜ   3 Ⓐ Ⓑ ● Ⓓ   6 ● Ⓚ Ⓛ Ⓜ   9 Ⓐ Ⓑ Ⓒ ●
18   1 Ⓐ Ⓑ ● Ⓓ   4 Ⓙ Ⓚ Ⓛ ●   7 Ⓐ ● Ⓒ Ⓓ   10 Ⓙ Ⓚ ● Ⓜ

Unit 4 Test

SAY: **Turn to the Unit 4 Test on page 18.**

Check to see that all students find the Unit 4 Test.

SAY: **In this test you will use the language skills that we have practiced in this unit. We will work the samples together befo you begin the test. Look at S1. Read the lines silently. Then darken the circle for the line that has a capitalization error. Darken the circle for *No mistakes* if there is no capitalization error.**

Allow students time to find and mark their answer.

SAY: **You should have darkened the circle for *A* because *uncle* should be capitalized when used with the name *Toby*.**

Check to see that all students have filled in the correct answer space. A students if they have any questions.

SAY: **Now look at S2. Read the lines silently. Then darken the circl for the line that has a punctuation error. Darken the circle for *No mistakes* if there is no punctuation error.**

Allow students time to find and mark their answer.

SAY: **You should have darkened the circle for *J* because it has a punctuation error. An initial that is part of a name should be followed by a period.**

Check to see that all students have filled in the correct answer space. A students if they have any questions.

SAY: **Now you will finish the test on your own. Read the directions for each section carefully. Do numbers 1 through 24 just as w did the samples. Read the lines carefully. Then darken the circle for each correct answer. When you come to the words *GO ON* at the bottom of page 18, continue working on the nex page. When you come to the word *STOP* at the bottom of pag 19, put your pencils down. You may now begin.**

Allow students time to find and mark their answers.

For questions 12–24, darken the circle for the line that has a punctuation error. Darken the circle for *No mistakes* if there is no punctuation error.

12 J When do you think men
    K and women will be able
    L to explore the planet Mars
    M *(No mistakes)*

13 A Chip Brownie and Cocoa are
    B the names that the Longs have
    C chosen for their three puppies.
    D *(No mistakes)*

14 J The saxophones tone is
    K deep and mellow. It's such a
    L smooth, relaxing sound.
    M *(No mistakes)*

15 A "I can't tell you how to get to
    B the civic center," said Rachel
    C "because I've never been there."
    D *(No mistakes)*

16 J Mom called the doctor this
    K morning. She made an
    L appointment for Wed morning.
    M *(No mistakes)*

17 A Have you ever wondered where
    B birds go in the winter? Many of
    C them fly to South, America.
    D *(No mistakes)*

18 J Dr. Martin Luther King, Jr, was
    K an important spokesman for
    L African Americans in the 1960s.
    M *(No mistakes)*

19 A What if? nobody obeyed the
    B traffic laws? There would sure
    C be a lot more car accidents!
    D *(No mistakes)*

20 J Kenneth's aunt and uncle won
    K a trip to Honolulu Hawaii.
    L They plan to go next month.
    M *(No mistakes)*

21 A   69 Mockingbird Lane
    B   Dallas, TX 72394
    C   September 15 1995
    D *(No mistakes)*

22 J Solar Action America
    K Dallas TX 72235
    L To whom it may concern:
    M *(No mistakes)*

23 A My class wants to learn about
    B solar power. Could someone from
    C your group speak to our class.
    D *(No mistakes)*

24 J   Yours truly
    K   Bernard Clark
    L   Harris School
    M *(No mistakes)*

STOP

SAY: **It is now time to stop. You have completed the Unit 4 Test. Make sure that you have carefully filled in your answer spaces and have completely erased any stray marks. Then put your pencils down.**

After the test has been scored, review the questions and answer choices with students. If students are having difficulty, provide them with additional practice items.

UNIT 5 Language Expression

Lesson 6: Determining Usage

Directions: Darken the circle for the line that has an error in the way the words are used. Darken the circle for *No mistakes* if all the words are used correctly.

TRY THIS	Read the sentences quietly to yourself. Listen for words or phrases that don't sound right. Look at each line carefully.

S1　A　When I see my dentist, she
　　B　reminds me that I must brush
　　C　my tooths after each meal.
　　D　*(No mistakes)*

 | THINK IT THROUGH | The correct answer is C. The correct plural form of *Tooth* is *teeth*, not *tooths*.

STOP

1　A　Everyone in our house
　　B　waked up at 3:00 A.M.
　　C　because the baby was crying.
　　D　*(No mistakes)*

2　J　The angry baby-sitter asked
　　K　the Martinez boys why they always
　　L　drop there coats on the floor.
　　M　*(No mistakes)*

3　A　When we went to the concert,
　　B　I and Ronni stood up and
　　C　clapped the whole time.
　　D　*(No mistakes)*

4　J　There weren't no prizes to
　　K　give to the winners that day.
　　L　They would be mailed later.
　　M　*(No mistakes)*

5　A　Willy was very excited about his
　　B　vacation to the mountains. He
　　C　had never went skiing.
　　D　*(No mistakes)*

6　J　On New Year's Day, we have
　　K　a big party. All of our friends
　　L　bring special desserts.
　　M　*(No mistakes)*

7　A　Mitchell and his older brothers
　　B　has been backpacking in the
　　C　Sawtooth Mountains in Idaho.
　　D　*(No mistakes)*

8　J　It takes a lot of cooperation
　　K　to build a house. The workers
　　L　they depend on one another.
　　M　*(No mistakes)*

9　A　Vanessa couldn't swim, so
　　B　she asked her best friend
　　C　Linda to learn her how.
　　D　*(No mistakes)*

10　J　The most commonest names
　　K　in the third-grade class
　　L　are John and Jennifer.
　　M　*(No mistakes)*

STOP

Answers
S1 Ⓐ Ⓑ ● Ⓓ
1 Ⓐ ● Ⓒ Ⓓ
2 Ⓙ Ⓚ ● Ⓜ
3 Ⓐ ● Ⓒ Ⓓ
4 ● Ⓚ Ⓛ Ⓜ
5 Ⓐ Ⓑ ● Ⓓ
6 Ⓙ Ⓚ Ⓛ ●
7 Ⓐ ● Ⓒ Ⓓ
8 Ⓙ Ⓚ ● Ⓜ
9 Ⓐ Ⓑ ● Ⓓ
10 ● Ⓚ Ⓛ Ⓜ

Level 11

20

UNIT 5 Language Expression

Lesson 6: Determining Usage

Language Skills: Determining the appropriate use of verbs, pronouns, adjectives, and adverbs within the context of sentences

SAY: **Turn to Lesson 6, Determining Usage, on page 20.**

Check to see that all students find Lesson 6.

SAY: **In Lesson 6 you will practice identifying the incorrect usage ⦁ words within sentences.**

Read the <u>Directions</u> to students.

SAY: **Now look at <u>Try This</u>.**

Read <u>Try This</u> to students.

SAY: **Now look at S1. Read each line carefully. Then darken the circle for the line that has an error in the way words are used. Darken the circle for *No mistakes* if all the words are used correctly.**

Allow students time to find and mark their answer.

SAY: **Now look at <u>Think It Through</u>.**

Read <u>Think It Through</u> to students. Check to see that all students have filled in the correct answer space. Ask students if they have any question⦁

SAY: **Now you will practice identifying the incorrect usage of word⦁ in more sentences. Do numbers 1 through 10 just as we did S⦁ When you come to the word *STOP* at the bottom of page 20, ⦁ put your pencils down. You may now begin.**

Allow students time to find and mark their answers.

Review the questions and answer choices with students. Discuss with th⦁ class why one answer is correct and the others are not correct. Also che⦁ to see that students have carefully filled in the answer spaces and have completely erased any stray marks.

Lesson 7: Choosing Correct Words and Phrases

Directions: Darken the circle for the word or words that best fit in the underlined part of the sentence. Darken the circle for *No change* if the sentence is correct as it is.

TRY THIS	First read the entire sentence. Ask yourself whether the underlined word or words make sense in the sentence. Then reread the sentence, using each answer choice in place of the underlined part of the sentence.

S1 When the doctor gave Jesse his shot, Jesse <u>clenches</u> his fist.

A will clench
B clenched
C clenching
D *(No change)*

 THINK IT THROUGH The correct answer is choice **B**. The word *gave* is in past tense and tells you that Jesse has already received the shot. Therefore, *clenches* also must be in the past tense. Jesse *clenched* his fist when he got a shot.

STOP

1 We all clapped loudly <u>while</u> the actors took their bows.

A since
B during
C where
D *(No change)*

2 <u>Having been arranging</u> flowers is something Sergio does well.

J To have arranged
K To be arranging
L Arranging
M *(No change)*

3 Zak didn't want his mother <u>to hearing</u> him mumbling.

A heard
B hear
C to hear
D *(No change)*

4 You can join us <u>because</u> you have made other plans.

J although
K if
L unless
M *(No change)*

5 They wanted to say good-bye <u>during</u> we left for vacation.

A until
B before
C while
D *(No change)*

6 The strong rains blinded the driver, who had <u>stopping</u>.

J for stopping
K stop
L to stop
M *(No change)*

STOP

Answers
S1 Ⓐ ● ⓒ Ⓓ   2 Ⓙ Ⓚ ● Ⓜ   4 Ⓙ Ⓚ ● Ⓜ   6 Ⓙ Ⓚ ● Ⓜ
1 Ⓐ Ⓑ ⓒ ●   3 Ⓐ Ⓑ ● Ⓓ   5 Ⓐ ● ⓒ Ⓓ

Level 11

21

Lesson 7: Choosing Correct Words and Phrases

Language Skill: Identifying the words and phrases that best fit in the context of a sentence

SAY: **Turn to Lesson 7, Choosing Correct Words and Phrases, on page 21.**

Check to see that all students find Lesson 7.

SAY: **In Lesson 7 you will practice identifying the word or words that best fit in a sentence.**

Read the <u>Directions</u> to students.

SAY: **Now look at <u>Try This</u>.**

Read <u>Try This</u> to students.

SAY: **Now look at S1. Read the sentence silently. Then darken the circle for the word or words that best fit in the underlined part of the sentence. Darken the circle for *No change* if the sentence is correct as it is.**

Allow students time to find and mark their answer.

SAY: **Now look at <u>Think It Through</u>.**

Read <u>Think It Through</u> to students. Check to see that all students have filled in the correct answer space. Ask students if they have any questions.

SAY: **Now you will practice identifying more words that best fit in a sentence. Do numbers 1 through 6 just as we did S1. When you come to the word *STOP* at the bottom of page 21, put your pencils down. You may now begin.**

Allow students time to find and mark their answers.

Review the questions and answer choices with students. Discuss with the class why one answer is correct and the others are not correct. Also check to see that students have carefully filled in the answer spaces and have completely erased any stray marks.

Lesson 8: Analyzing Paragraphs

Directions: Darken the circle for the correct answer. Darken the circle for *No change* if the sentence is correct as it is.

TRY THIS | Read the paragraph carefully. Then read the question and each answer choice before choosing your answer. Check your answers by looking back at the paragraph.

S1

¹ Hopi Indians lived in the southwest part of the United States, in what is now Arizona. ² They <u>have been making</u> most of what they needed to live. ³ They created pottery for dishes and grew cotton, which they used to make clothing. ⁴ They also were always <u>growing</u> their own crops for food. ⁵ Farming was difficult, however, because the land was dry. ⁶ Today, Arizona is known for its hot desert climate. ⁷ Since the Hopi were religious people, they prayed to their gods for the rain they needed.

Which sentence does <u>not</u> belong in the paragraph?

A Sentence 2   C Sentence 5

B Sentence 4   D Sentence 6

 THINK IT THROUGH The correct answer is D. The topic of the paragraph is the Hopi Indians. Sentence 6 describes Arizona's climate, not the Hopi Indians. It does <u>not</u> belong in the paragraph.

STOP

Use the paragraph in S1 to answer questions 1–4.

1 Choose the best opening sentence for this paragraph.

A While I was on vacation, I visited a Native American reservation.

B In ancient times, many Native American groups lived in North America.

C I have learned a lot about Native Americans in social studies class.

D Many Hopi Indians still live in Arizona today.

2 What is the best way to write the underlined part of sentence 2?

J were making

K made

L will be making

M *(No change)*

3 What is the best way to write the underlined part of sentence 4?

A grew

B were planning to grow

C will be eating

D *(No change)*

4 What is the best concluding sentence for this paragraph?

J The Hopi village of Oraibi is one of the oldest continuously inhabited villages in the United States.

K The Hopi were always a proud, independent people.

L The Hopi Indians had always preferred to live in a wet climate.

M Today the Hopi still farm the dry land, and they make money by selling their handmade pottery, jewelry, and baskets.

GO ON

Level 11

Answers

S1 Ⓐ Ⓑ Ⓒ ●   2 Ⓙ ● Ⓛ Ⓜ   4 Ⓙ Ⓚ Ⓛ ●

22   1 Ⓐ ● Ⓒ Ⓓ   3 ● Ⓑ Ⓒ Ⓓ

Lesson 8: Analyzing Paragraphs

Language Skills: Determining the topic and supporting details of a paragraph; identifying information that does not belong in a paragraph; determining word usage in the context of a paragraph

SAY: **Turn to Lesson 8, Analyzing Paragraphs, on page 22.**

Check to see that all students find Lesson 8.

SAY: **In Lesson 8 you will practice analyzing paragraphs.**

Read the <u>Directions</u> to students.

SAY: **Now look at <u>Try This</u>.**

Read <u>Try This</u> to students.

SAY: **Now look at S1. Read the paragraph silently. Then read the question and answer choices carefully. Darken the circle for the choice that shows the sentence that does <u>not</u> belong in the paragraph.**

Allow students time to find and mark their answer.

SAY: **Now look at <u>Think It Through</u>.**

Read <u>Think It Through</u> to students. Check to see that all students have filled in the correct answer space. Ask students if they have any questions.

SAY: **Now you will practice further analyzing the paragraph. Do numbers 1 through 4 just as we did S1. When you come to the words *GO ON* at the bottom of page 22, go to page 23. For questions 5 and 6, read each question and the paragraph answer choices. Then choose the answer that best fits the given situation. When you come to the word *STOP* at the bottom of page 23, put your pencils down. You may now begin.**

Allow students time to find and mark their answers.

For questions 5 and 6, choose the answer that best fits the given situation.

5 Which of the following would be most appropriate in a thank-you note for a birthday present?

A | Thank you for the birthday gift. The sweater fits perfectly, but I don't much like the pants. Can they be exchanged?

B | Thank you for the beautiful sweater and pants. I really like the colors in the sweater, and the pants are a perfect fit.

C | Birthday gifts are always wonderful. Mostly, I like everything I get. Why don't you come by and see me in the sweater and pants you gave me for my birthday?

D | Do you remember your best birthday party? Mine was last week. I received many presents. My favorite was a new bike. By the way, thank you for your gift.

6 Which of the following would be most appropriate in a letter requesting information about a state park?

J | My family needs to reserve about six camping spaces. We want to have a reunion in Palm Lake State Park in July. Tell me how to make reservations.

K | Palm Lake State Park is really pretty. I was there last year with my aunt and uncle. We want to reserve six camping spaces for July 10. They have to be next to each other.

L | My family plans to have a reunion in Palm Lake State Park on July 10. Please send me information about your park. I would like to make reservations for six camping spaces, preferably next to one another.

M | What's the weather like in your park in July? My family's thinking about going there for a reunion, but we don't want to go if it's too hot and there's no place to swim.

STOP

Answers
5 Ⓐ ● Ⓒ Ⓓ
6 Ⓙ Ⓚ ● Ⓜ

Level 11

23

Review the questions and answer choices with students. Discuss with the class why one answer is correct and the others are not correct. Also check to see that students have carefully filled in the answer spaces and have completely erased any stray marks.

Lesson 9: Expressing Ideas Clearly

Directions: Darken the circle for the sentence or sentences that express the idea most clearly.

> **TRY THIS**
> Read each answer choice carefully. Look for the sentence or sentences that are clear and make the most sense.

S1
  A The movie *Dick Tracy* is certainly better than *Batman*.
  B Than *Batman*, the movie *Dick Tracy* is better, certainly.
  C Certainly better than *Batman*, the movie is *Dick Tracy*.
  D *Dick Tracy*, the movie, certainly than *Batman* is better.

> **THINK IT THROUGH**
> The correct answer is A. It is the only complete sentence. It is clear and makes sense. The other choices do not make sense.

STOP

1
  A On the piano, Jake wanted to play a song that was out of tune.
  B Jack wanted to play a song on the piano, but it was out of tune.
  C Jake, out of tune, wanted to play a song on the piano.
  D Even though out of tune, Jack wanted to play a song on the piano.

2
  J A choice of grilled fish or ribs for dinner is what we have.
  K For dinner, we have grilled fish or ribs, a choice.
  L We have for dinner a choice of grilled fish or a choice of ribs.
  M For dinner, we have a choice of grilled fish or ribs.

3
  A Raccoons have a habit of washing their hands before eating.
  B Before eating, raccoons wash their hands as a habit.
  C It's a habit for raccoons before eating to wash their hands.
  D Washing their hands is a habit of raccoons before eating.

4
  J Uncle Alfredo bought a computer for our family that was expensive.
  K Although expensive, Uncle Alfredo bought a computer for our family.
  L Uncle Alfredo bought an expensive computer for our family.
  M Being expensive, our family got a computer from Uncle Alfredo.

STOP

Level 11

Answers
S1 ● Ⓑ Ⓒ Ⓓ   2 Ⓙ Ⓚ Ⓛ ●   4 Ⓙ Ⓚ ● Ⓜ
24 1 Ⓐ ● Ⓒ Ⓓ   3 ● Ⓑ Ⓒ Ⓓ

Lesson 9: Expressing Ideas Clearly

Language Skill: Identifying sentences that are the clearest, most concise and best examples of effective writing

SAY: **Turn to Lesson 9, Expressing Ideas Clearly, on page 24.**

Check to see that all students find Lesson 9.

SAY: **In Lesson 9 you will practice identifying the sentence or sentences that express the idea most clearly.**

Read the <u>Directions</u> to students.

SAY: **Now look at <u>Try This</u>.**

Read <u>Try This</u> to students.

SAY: **Now look at S1. Read the sentences silently. Then darken the circle for the choice that shows the sentence or sentences that express the idea most clearly.**

Allow students time to find and mark their answer.

SAY: **Now look at <u>Think It Through</u>.**

Read <u>Think It Through</u> to students. Check to see that all students have filled in the correct answer space. Ask students if they have any questions.

SAY: **Now you will practice identifying more sentences that express an idea most clearly. Do numbers 1 through 4 just as we did S1. When you come to the word *STOP* at the bottom of page 24, put your pencils down. You may now begin.**

Allow students time to find and mark their answers.

Review the questions and answer choices with students. Discuss with the class why one answer is correct and the others are not correct. Also check to see that students have carefully filled in the answer spaces and have completely erased any stray marks.

Unit 5 Test

S1 A My mother and I like to
    B goes to the movies together
    C on Saturday afternoon.
    D (No mistakes)

STOP

For questions 1–11, darken the circle for the line that has an error in the way the words are used. Darken the circle for *No mistakes* if all the words are used correctly.

1 A Reading a book in the
   B warm sunshine is the
   C most peaceful activity I no.
   D (No mistakes)

2 J On Thursday I gave my
   K brother two dollars. A day
   L later, he had spent it all!
   M (No mistakes)

3 A Washington it is the only
   B state in the United States
   C named for a President.
   D (No mistakes)

4 J Izumi set up a lemonade
   K stand at the carnival, but hardly
   L nobody didn't want to buy any.
   M (No mistakes)

5 A Some California redwood
   B trees are so large, you
   C might could drive through them.
   D (No mistakes)

6 J My family camped in the
   K Grand Canyon last summer.
   L It is the most uniquest place!
   M (No mistakes)

7 A I and my baby brother had
   B to keep quiet while our father
   C was reading the newspaper.
   D (No mistakes)

8 J Animals once did all the work
   K that machines do today. Oxes
   L and horses pulled heavy loads.
   M (No mistakes)

9 A Every afternoon after school,
   B my friends and I go to the
   C neighborhood park to play soccer.
   D (No mistakes)

10 J When the lifeguard was
   K stinged by the hornet, he
   L jumped into the pool for relief.
   M (No mistakes)

11 A When I heard the bell for
   B school, I runned so fast that
   C I slipped and fell.
   D (No mistakes)

GO ON

Answers
S1 Ⓐ ● Ⓒ Ⓓ   3 ● Ⓑ Ⓒ Ⓓ   6 Ⓙ Ⓚ ● Ⓜ   9 Ⓐ Ⓑ Ⓒ ●
1 Ⓐ Ⓑ ● Ⓓ   4 Ⓙ Ⓚ ● Ⓜ   7 ● Ⓑ Ⓒ Ⓓ   10 Ⓙ Ⓚ ● Ⓜ
2 Ⓙ Ⓚ ● Ⓜ   5 Ⓐ Ⓑ ● Ⓓ   8 Ⓙ ● Ⓛ Ⓜ   11 Ⓐ ● Ⓒ Ⓓ

Unit 5 Test

SAY: **Turn to the Unit 5 Test on page 25.**

Check to see that all students find the Unit 5 Test.

SAY: **In this test you will use the language skills that we have practiced in this unit. This test is divided into five parts. We will work the sample together before you begin the test. Look at S1. Read the answer choices carefully. Then darken the circle for the line that has an error in the way words are used. Darken the circle for *No mistakes* if all the words are used correctly.**

Allow students time to find and mark their answer.

SAY: **You should have darkened the circle for *B* because *mother and I* is a plural subject and require the plural verb form, *go*.**

Check to see that all students have filled in the correct answer space. Ask students if they have any questions.

SAY: **Now you will finish the test on your own. Read the directions for each section carefully. Do numbers 1 through 32 just as we did the sample. Read the questions and answer choices carefully. Then darken the circle for each correct answer. When you come to the words *GO ON* at the bottom of a page, continue working on the next page. When you come to the word *STOP* at the bottom of page 28, put your pencils down. You may now begin.**

Allow students time to find and mark their answers.

S1   A My mother and I like to
      B goes to the movies together
      C on Saturday afternoon.
      D *(No mistakes)*

STOP

For questions 1–11, darken the circle for the line that has an error in the way the words are used. Darken the circle for *No mistakes* if all the words are used correctly.

1   A Reading a book in the
    B warm sunshine is the
    C most peaceful activity I no.
    D *(No mistakes)*

2   J On Thursday I gave my
    K brother two dollars. A day
    L later, he had spended it all!
    M *(No mistakes)*

3   A Washington it is the only
    B state in the United States
    C named for a President.
    D *(No mistakes)*

4   J Izumi set up a lemonade
    K stand at the carnival, but hardly
    L nobody didn't want to buy any.
    M *(No mistakes)*

5   A Some California redwood
    B trees are so large, you
    C might could drive through them.
    D *(No mistakes)*

6   J My family camped in the
    K Grand Canyon last summer.
    L It is the most uniquest place!
    M *(No mistakes)*

7   A I and my baby brother had
    B to keep quiet while our father
    C was reading the newspaper.
    D *(No mistakes)*

8   J Animals once did all the work
    K that machines do today. Oxes
    L and horses pulled heavy loads.
    M *(No mistakes)*

9   A Every afternoon after school,
    B my friends and I go to the
    C neighborhood park to play soccer.
    D *(No mistakes)*

10   J When the lifeguard was
     K stinged by the hornet, he
     L jumped into the pool for relief.
     M *(No mistakes)*

11   A When I heard the bell for
     B school, I runned so fast that
     C I slipped and fell.
     D *(No mistakes)*

GO ON

Answers

S1 Ⓐ ● Ⓒ Ⓓ   3 ● Ⓑ Ⓒ Ⓓ   6 Ⓙ Ⓚ ● Ⓜ   9 Ⓐ Ⓑ Ⓒ ●
1 Ⓐ Ⓑ ● Ⓓ   4 Ⓙ Ⓚ ● Ⓜ   7 ● Ⓑ Ⓒ Ⓓ   10 Ⓙ ● Ⓛ Ⓜ
2 Ⓙ Ⓚ ● Ⓜ   5 Ⓐ Ⓑ ● Ⓓ   8 Ⓙ ● Ⓛ Ⓜ   11 Ⓐ ● Ⓒ Ⓓ

For questions 12–21, darken the circle for the word or words that best fit in the underlined part of the sentence. Darken the circle for *No change* if the sentence is correct as it is.

12 <u>Learning</u> first aid is a good idea for everybody.

J To learn

K The learning of

L To have learned

M *(No change)*

13 Inez's grandfather <u>will carve</u> wooden animals for many years now.

A is carving

B has been carving

C carves

D *(No change)*

14 Mario couldn't see the movie <u>that</u> he put his glasses on.

J where

K except

L until

M *(No change)*

15 I'll drive you home <u>because</u> you show me how to get there.

A although

B if

C unless

D *(No change)*

16 When Donald grows up, he knows he <u>becomes</u> a musician.

J is becoming

K will become

L has become

M *(No change)*

17 Last year on their trip, the Cub Scouts <u>hiked</u> ten miles.

A are hiking

B will hike

C have hiked

D *(No change)*

18 Michiko is <u>smiling</u> and thanked me for the birthday gift.

J smiles

K smiled

L have smiled

M *(No change)*

19 If we go to the mall, I'm sure we <u>have spent</u> too much money.

A had spent

B will be spending

C will spend

D *(No change)*

20 Would you rather play catch <u>not</u> swim in the pool?

J or

K before

L and

M *(No change)*

21 Ed has been missing his parents <u>because</u> the minute they left.

A during

B since

C when

D *(No change)*

GO ON

Level 11

26

For questions 22–25, read the paragraph. Then darken the circle for each correct answer. Darken the circle for *No change* if the sentence is correct as it is.

> [1] Our neighborhood park is always filled with people. [2] Some parks have refreshment stands. [3] Older people who are not children sit on the benches and read their newspapers early in the morning. [4] The slide and swings are a favorite place for young children to play. [5] Parents often push their babies in strollers around the park. [6] After school and on weekends, older kids play baseball or basketball.

22 Choose the best way to write the underlined part of sentence 3.

    J Teenagers

    K People, older than children,

    L Adults

    M *(No change)*

23 What is the best way to write the underlined part of sentence 5?

    A often pushing

    B are often pushing

    C pushing, often

    D *(No change)*

24 What is the best concluding sentence to add to this paragraph?

    J Most cities have large public parks.

    K The people at our park are always friendly.

    L A park is a great place to be!

    M Some people meet friends at the park.

25 Which sentence should be left out of the paragraph?

    A Sentence 2

    B Sentence 3

    C Sentence 4

    D Sentence 6

For question 26, choose the answer that best fits the given situation.

26 Which would be most appropriate in a thank-you letter to a classroom visitor?

    J I really enjoyed listening to you talk about writing your books. Our librarian has ordered the latest one, and I can't wait to read it. Thanks for coming to our class!

    K Your talk was pretty interesting, but I think you should have talked more about *Tales of the Palmetto*. That was the only book I really wanted to hear about.

    L I want to be a musician when I grow up. Writing and reading have always bored me, so I've never read your books. But thanks for visiting our class.

    M How do you come up with the ideas for your books? I want to be a writer, so please write as soon as you can to let me know how you do it.

Level 11

Answers

22 Ⓙ Ⓚ ● Ⓜ   24 Ⓙ Ⓚ ● Ⓜ   26 ● Ⓚ Ⓛ Ⓜ

23 Ⓐ Ⓑ Ⓒ ●   25 ● Ⓑ Ⓒ Ⓓ

27

For questions 27–32, darken the circle for the sentence or sentences that express the idea most clearly.

27   A   The argument ending between Hamid and Will.
     B   When he left, the argument between Hamid and Will ended.
     C   Hamid and Will ended their argument when he left.
     D   The argument between Hamid and Will ended when Hamid left.

28   J   Since the book on the table, Concepción wanted it.
     K   Concepción saw the book and wanted it on the table.
     L   Concepción wanted the book that was on the table.
     M   Concepción wanted the book it was on the table.

29   A   Formed billions of years ago, Earth, our planet.
     B   Our planet Earth was formed billions of years ago.
     C   Billions of years ago, Earth our planet, forming.
     D   Earth, our planet. It was formed billions of years ago.

30   J   Sandra is always early, arriving before any other student.
     K   Sandra is always early and first before any other student arrives.
     L   Before any other student, Sandra, arriving early, comes first.
     M   Being always first, Sandra comes early before any other student.

31   A   So beautiful Akiko wanted it framed, she painted a picture.
     B   Akiko painted a beautiful picture. And wanted it framed.
     C   Akiko painting a picture, she wanted to frame it.
     D   Akiko painted a beautiful picture and wanted to frame it.

32   J   With pride, Nicholas was proud of himself at his graduation.
     K   At his graduation, Nicholas had much pride in himself.
     L   Nicholas was very proud of himself at his graduation.
     M   Proud of himself, Nicholas at his graduation.

STOP

Answers

27 Ⓐ Ⓑ Ⓒ ●	29 Ⓐ ● Ⓒ Ⓓ	31 Ⓐ Ⓑ Ⓒ ●
28 Ⓙ Ⓚ ● Ⓜ	30 ● Ⓚ Ⓛ Ⓜ	32 Ⓙ Ⓚ ● Ⓜ

28

It is now time to stop. You have completed the Unit 5 Test. Make sure that you have carefully filled in your answer spaces and have completely erased any stray marks. Then put your pencils down.

After the test has been scored, review the questions and answer choices with students. If students are having difficulty, provide them with additional practice.

UNIT 6 Math Concepts and Estimation

Lesson 10: Understanding Numeration

Directions: Darken the circle for the correct answer.

> **TRY THIS** Read each question twice before choosing your answer. Be sure to think about which numbers stand for ones, tens, hundreds, and so on.

S1 In which of the following numbers does the 6 stand for 6 hundreds?

A 246   C 637

B 468   D 6,052

> **THINK IT THROUGH** The correct answer is C. The 6 is in the hundreds place, the 3 is in the tens place, and the 7 is in the ones place.

STOP

1 Which numeral has the greatest value?

| 1435 | 1543 | 3145 | 1354 | 4315 |

A 1543

B 4315

C 3145

D 1354

2 What is another way to write thirty thousand eight?

J 30,008

K 30,080

L 30,088

M 38,000

3 Jill is sixth in line. How many persons are in front of her?

A 4   C 6

B 5   D 7

4 By how much does the value change, if the 9 in 2910 is changed to a 4?

J 5

K 50

L 400

M 500

5 What should replace the △ in the multiplication problem shown here?

A 2

B 3

C 4

D 5

$$
\begin{array}{r}
314 \\
\times\, 42 \\
\hline
628 \\
12\triangle6 \\
\hline
13\square88
\end{array}
$$

6 Which numeral has a value between 8250 and 8930?

J 8160   L 8888

K 8229   M 8949

STOP

Answers

S1 Ⓐ Ⓑ ● Ⓓ   2 ● Ⓚ Ⓛ Ⓜ   4 Ⓙ Ⓚ Ⓛ ●   6 Ⓙ Ⓚ ● Ⓜ

1 Ⓐ ● Ⓒ Ⓓ   3 Ⓐ ● Ⓒ Ⓓ   5 Ⓐ Ⓑ Ⓒ ●

Level 11

29

UNIT 6: Math Concepts and Estimation

Lesson 10: Understanding Numeration

Mathematics Skills: Identifying place value, fractional parts, multiples of numbers; estimating; understanding number theory and relationships

SAY: **Turn to Lesson 10, Understanding Numeration, on page 29.**

Check to see that all students find Lesson 10.

Distribute scratch paper to students. Tell them they may use the scratch paper to work the problems.

SAY: **In Lesson 10 you will demonstrate your understanding of number theory and number relationships.**

Read the <u>Directions</u> to students.

SAY: **Now look at <u>Try This</u>.**

Read <u>Try This</u> to students.

SAY: **Now look at S1. You are asked to identify the number in which 6 stands for 6 hundreds. Look at the choices carefully. Then darken the circle for the correct answer.**

Allow students time to find and mark their answer.

SAY: **Now look at <u>Think It Through</u>.**

Read <u>Think It Through</u> to students. Check to see that all students have filled in the correct answer space. Ask students if they have any questions.

SAY: **Now you will practice answering more numeration questions. Do numbers 1 through 6 just as we did S1. When you come to the word *STOP* at the bottom of page 29, put your pencils down. You may now begin.**

Allow students time to find and mark their answers.

Review the questions and answer choices with students. Discuss with the class why one answer is correct and the others are not correct. Also check to see that students have carefully filled in the answer spaces and have completely erased any stray marks.

Lesson 11: Working with Number Sentences

Directions: Darken the circle for the correct answer.

TRY THIS Only one answer will make each number sentence correct. Check each answer carefully by replacing the missing numeral with each answer choice until you obtain a correct statement.

S1 What value for ☐ makes this number sentence correct?

$\square + 2 = 9$

A 11　　　C 20
B 18　　　D 27

THINK IT THROUGH The correct answer is B. Test each possible answer by replacing the ☐ in the number sentence with each choice. By doing this, you will see that 18 is the only numeral that makes the number sentence correct.

STOP

---

1 Which numeral will make this number sentence true?

$(3 \times \square) - 3 = 18$

A 5　　　C 7
B 6　　　D 8

2 Which symbol would replace the ◯ in the following number sentence?

$3 \times 5 = 8 \bigcirc 7$

J +　　　L ×
K −　　　M ÷

3 How could the following number sentence be solved?

$14 \div \square = 7$

A Divide 14 by 7
B Add 14 and 7
C Multiply 14 times 7
D Subtract 7 from 14

4 What value for ☐ will make the following number sentence true?

$(0 + 6) + 3 = (3 + 0) + \square$

J 0　　　L 6
K 3　　　M 9

5 How could the following number sentence be solved?

$12 + \square = 24$

A Add 24 and 12
B Multiply 24 times 12
C Subtract 12 from 24
D Divide 24 by 12

6 What would replace the ☐ to make the number sentence true?

$(4 + 5) + 2 = (5 + \square) + 2$

J 0　　　L 4
K 2　　　M 5

STOP
Level 11

Answers
S1 Ⓐ ● Ⓒ Ⓓ　　2 ● Ⓚ Ⓛ Ⓜ　　4 Ⓙ Ⓚ ● Ⓜ　　6 Ⓙ Ⓚ ● Ⓜ
30　1 Ⓐ Ⓑ ● Ⓓ　　3 ● Ⓑ Ⓒ Ⓓ　　5 Ⓐ Ⓑ ● Ⓓ

Lesson 11: Working with Number Sentences

Mathematics Skill: Solving number sentences

SAY: **Turn to Lesson 11, Working with Number Sentences, on page 30.**

Check to see that all students find Lesson 11.

Distribute scratch paper to students. Tell them they may use the scratch paper to work the problems.

SAY: **In Lesson 11 you will practice solving number sentences.**

Read the Directions to students.

SAY: **Now look at Try This.**

Read Try This to students.

SAY: **Now look at S1. You are asked to identify the missing value that would make the number sentence correct. Look at the choices carefully. Then darken the circle for the correct answer.**

Allow students time to find and mark their answer.

SAY: **Now look at Think It Through.**

Read Think It Through to students. Check to see that all students have filled in the correct answer space. Ask students if they have any questions.

SAY: **Now you will practice solving more number sentences. Do numbers 1 through 6 just as we did S1. When you come to the word STOP at the bottom of page 30, put your pencils down. You may now begin.**

Allow students time to find and mark their answers.

Review the questions and answer choices with students. Discuss with the class why one answer is correct and the others are not correct. Also check to see that students have carefully filled in the answer spaces and have completely erased any stray marks.

Lesson 12: Using Probability and Statistics

Directions: Darken the circle for the correct answer.

> **TRY THIS**
> To find the average (mean) of a set of numbers, first add the numbers. Then divide the sum by the number of addends in the set.

S1 What is the average (mean) of this set of numbers {10, 9, 14, 11}?

A 9
B 11
C 44
D 55

> **THINK IT THROUGH**
> The correct answer is B. The sum of the set of numbers is 44, and 44 ÷ 4 = 11.

STOP

1 With his eyes closed, which card will Cal most likely pick from the following cards?

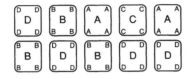

A A   C C
B B   D D

2 What is the average (mean) of this set of numbers {15, 17, 21, 23}?

J 15   L 19
K 17   M 21

3 Which set of numbers shown here has the greatest average (mean)?

A {3, 4, 7}
B {1, 8, 2}
C {9, 7, 5}
D {5, 4, 5}

4 If Keiko spins the spinner, on which number is the spinner most likely to stop?

J 1
K 2
L 3
M 4

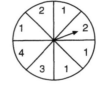

5 A red, a white, and a blue marble are in a box. If the blue marble is picked first, how many different ways can the other marbles be picked?

A 1
B 2
C 3
D 4

6 Which set of numbers shown here has the greatest average (mean)?

J {2, 9, 10}
K {7, 9, 15}
L {4, 10, 10}
M {10, 5, 6}

STOP

Level 11

Answers
S1 Ⓐ ● Ⓒ Ⓓ   2 Ⓙ Ⓚ ● Ⓜ   4 ● Ⓚ Ⓛ Ⓜ   6 Ⓙ ● Ⓛ Ⓜ
1 Ⓐ Ⓑ Ⓒ ●   3 Ⓐ Ⓑ ● Ⓓ   5 Ⓐ ● Ⓒ Ⓓ

31

Lesson 12: Using Probability and Statistics

Mathematics Skills: Understanding probability and statistics concepts; applying probability and statistics concepts in problem solving

SAY: **Turn to Lesson 12, Using Probability and Statistics, on page 31.**

Check to see that all students find Lesson 12.

Distribute scratch paper to students. Tell them they may use the scratch paper to work the problems.

SAY: **In Lesson 12 you will practice solving problems of probability and statistics.**

Read the <u>Directions</u> to students.

SAY: **Now look at <u>Try This</u>.**

Read <u>Try This</u> to students.

SAY: **Now look at S1. You are asked to find the average (mean) of four numbers. Find the solution. Then darken the circle for the correct answer.**

Allow students time to find and mark their answer.

SAY: **Now look at <u>Think It Through</u>.**

Read <u>Think It Through</u> to students. Check to see that all students have filled in the correct answer space. Ask students if they have any questions.

SAY: **Now you will practice solving more problems of probability and statistics. Do numbers 1 through 6 just as we did S1. When you come to the word _STOP_ at the bottom of page 31, put your pencils down. You may now begin.**

Allow students time to find and mark their answers.

Review the questions and answer choices with students. Discuss with the class why one answer is correct and the others are not correct. Also check to see that students have carefully filled in the answer spaces and have completely erased any stray marks.

Lesson 13: Using Measurement and Geometry

Directions: Darken the circle for the correct answer.

| TRY THIS | Use the objects shown or named to help you answer each question. |

S1 What units are used to measure length on a ruler?

   A Degrees

   B Kilograms

   C Centimeters

   D Liters

THINK IT THROUGH The correct answer is C. Degrees are used to measure temperature, kilograms are used to measure mass, and liters are used to measure capacity.

STOP

---

1 Which figure is <u>not</u> a rectangle?

  A   C

  B   D

2 Which unit of measurement is best to use to describe the weight of a bucket of sand?

   J Feet   L Liters

   K Miles   M Pounds

3 The figure shown here has $\frac{4}{10}$ of its area shaded. How much is <u>not</u> shaded?

  A $\frac{1}{2}$ C $\frac{4}{6}$

  B $\frac{6}{10}$ D $\frac{4}{10}$

4 One liter is closest in value to which measurement?

   J 1 gram   L 1 gallon

   K 1 quart   M 1 meter

5 Aunt Lila's rose garden is in the shape of a square. **How many feet of edging does she need to go around the entire garden?**

14 ft.

  A 14 feet   C 56 feet

  B 28 feet   D 196 feet

6 What time will it be in three and one-half hours, if it is 10:30 A.M. now?

   J 1:30 P.M.   L 2:30 P.M.

   K 2:00 P.M.   M 3:30 P.M.

STOP

Level 11

Answers

S1 Ⓐ Ⓑ ● Ⓓ   2 Ⓙ Ⓚ Ⓛ ●   4 Ⓙ ● Ⓛ Ⓜ   6 Ⓙ ● Ⓛ Ⓜ

32   1 Ⓐ Ⓑ ● Ⓓ   3 Ⓐ ● Ⓒ Ⓓ   5 Ⓐ Ⓑ ● Ⓓ

Lesson 13: Using Measurement and Geometry

Mathematics Skills: Working with customary and metric units of length, quantity, height, and weight; identifying congruent and similar figures; determining time, area, and perimeter of plane figures; recognizing three-dimensional forms; identifying angles and line segments

SAY: **Turn to Lesson 13, Using Measurement and Geometry, on page 32.**

Check to see that all students find Lesson 13.

Distribute scratch paper to students. Tell them they may use the scratch paper to work the problems.

SAY: **In Lesson 13 you will practice solving problems about measurement and shape.**

Read the <u>Directions</u> to students.

SAY: **Now look at <u>Try This</u>.**

Read <u>Try This</u> to students.

SAY: **Now look at S1. You are asked to name the units that are used to measure length on a ruler. Read the answer choices carefully. Then darken the circle for the correct answer.**

Allow students time to find and mark their answer.

SAY: **Now look at <u>Think It Through</u>.**

Read <u>Think It Through</u> to students. Check to see that all students have filled in the correct answer space. Ask students if they have any questions.

SAY: **Now you will practice solving more problems about measurement and shape. Do numbers 1 through 6 just as we did S1. When you come to the word *STOP* at the bottom of page 32, put your pencils down. You may now begin.**

Allow students time to find and mark their answers.

Review the questions and answer choices with students. Discuss with the class why one answer is correct and the others are not correct. Also check to see that students have carefully filled in the answer spaces and have completely erased any stray marks.

Lesson 14: Using Estimation

Directions: Darken the circle for the correct answer.

TRY THIS
When you estimate answers, round the numbers. For some problems, there are no exact answers. Then you should take your best guess. You can check your answer by using the numbers given in the problem.

S1 The closest estimate of 3819 + 5924 is _____.

A 3000 + 5000   C 4000 + 5000
B 3000 + 6000   D 4000 + 6000

THINK IT THROUGH
The correct answer is D. Round 3819 to 4000 and round 5924 to 6000.

STOP

1 Jed's father chose 5 videos to rent. The closest estimate of the total cost of renting the 5 videos is _____.

Video Prices:
$3.00
$3.75
$5.50
$1.75
$2.75

A $14   C $18
B $15   D $20

2 The closest estimate of 750 ÷ 8 is _____.

J 9   L 900
K 90   M 9000

3 The closest estimate of 455 + 320 + 878 is _____.

A 400 + 300 + 800
B 400 + 300 + 900
C 500 + 300 + 800
D 500 + 300 + 900

4 The closest estimate of $17.78 − $4.18 is _____.

J $12   L $14
K $13   M $15

5 Each week John saves $6.80 from his paper route. **The closest estimate of the amount John will save in 19 weeks is _____.**

A $14   C $1400
B $140   D $14,000

6 The closest estimate of 715 × 6 is between _____.

J 3500 and 3800
K 4000 and 4200
L 4200 and 4400
M 4400 and 4600

STOP

Level 11

Answers
S1 Ⓐ Ⓑ Ⓒ ●   2 Ⓙ ● Ⓛ Ⓜ   4 Ⓙ Ⓚ ● Ⓜ   6 Ⓙ Ⓚ ● Ⓜ
1 Ⓐ Ⓑ ● Ⓓ   3 Ⓐ Ⓑ Ⓒ ●   5 Ⓐ ● Ⓒ Ⓓ

33

Lesson 14: Using Estimation

Mathematics Skill: Estimating

SAY: **Turn to Lesson 14, Using Estimation, on page 33.**

Check to see that all students find Lesson 14.

Do not distribute scratch paper to students. Tell them they should work the problems in their head.

SAY: **In Lesson 14 you will practice estimating answers to problem**

Read the <u>Directions</u> to students.

SAY: **Now look at <u>Try This</u>.**

Read <u>Try This</u> to students.

SAY: **Now look at S1. You are asked to estimate the answer to an addition problem. Read the answer choices carefully. Then darken the circle for the correct answer.**

Allow students time to find and mark their answer.

SAY: **Now look at <u>Think It Through</u>.**

Read <u>Think It Through</u> to students. Check to see that all students have filled in the correct answer space. Ask students if they have any question

SAY: **Now you will practice estimating answers to more problems. Do numbers 1 through 6 just as we did S1. When you come to the word *STOP* at the bottom of page 33, put your pencils down. You may now begin.**

Allow students time to find and mark their answers.

Review the questions and answer choices with students. Discuss with the class why one answer is correct and the others are not correct. Also che to see that students have carefully filled in the answer spaces and have completely erased any stray marks.

═══════════════════ **Unit 6 Test** ═══════════════════

S1 What is the value of the 6 in 32.65?

   A 6 tenths

   B 6 ones

   C 6 tens

   D 6 hundredths

                                 STOP

For questions 1–33, darken the circle for the correct answer.

1 Which numeral has the greatest value?

6435	6543	3645	6354	4365

   A 6543

   B 4365

   C 3645

   D 6354

2 What is another name for twenty-three thousand eighty?

   J 23,008

   K 23,080

   L 23,088

   M 23,800

3 What should replace the △ in the multiplication problem below?

   A 2

   B 3

   C 4

   D 5

            412

          × 43

        1236

       16△8

       17☐16

4 The figure shown here demonstrates that $\frac{1}{4}$ is the same as what number?

   J $\frac{3}{6}$

   K $\frac{2}{8}$

   L $\frac{2}{4}$

   M $\frac{4}{8}$

5 Jenna is fourth in line to ride the ferris wheel. How many persons are in front of her?

   A 3   C 5

   B 4   D 6

6 By how much does the value change if the 5 in 8572 is changed to a 9?

   J 4

   K 40

   L 400

   M 500

7 What fraction of the set of shapes are triangles?

   A $\frac{2}{8}$ C $\frac{2}{6}$

   B $\frac{6}{8}$ D $\frac{8}{2}$

8 What is another way to write sixty-four hundredths?

   J 0.064

   K 0.64

   L 6.4

   M 6400

                                GO ON

                                Level 11

Answers

34

S1 ● Ⓑ Ⓒ Ⓓ   **2** Ⓙ ● Ⓛ Ⓜ   **4** Ⓙ ● Ⓛ Ⓜ   **6** Ⓙ Ⓚ ● Ⓜ   **8** Ⓙ ● Ⓛ Ⓜ

1 ● Ⓑ Ⓒ Ⓓ   **3** Ⓐ Ⓑ ● Ⓓ   **5** ● Ⓑ Ⓒ Ⓓ   **7** Ⓐ ● Ⓒ Ⓓ

Unit 6 Test

SAY: **Turn to the Unit 6 Test on page 34.**

Check to see that all students find the Unit 6 Test.

Distribute scratch paper to students. Tell them they may use the scratch paper to work all problems except numbers 25 through 33 on page 37. These are estimation problems that students should work in their heads.

SAY: **In this test you will use the mathematics skills that we have practiced in this unit. Look at S1. You are asked to find the value of 6 in the number 32.65. Darken the circle for the correct answer.**

Allow students time to find and mark their answer.

SAY: **You should have darkened the circle for _A_ because the _6_ is in the _tenths_ place.**

Check to see that all students have filled in the correct answer space. Ask students if they have any questions.

SAY: **Now you will finish the test on your own. Put your finger on number 1. Do numbers 1 through 33 just as we did S1. Read the problems and answer choices carefully. Then darken the circle for each correct answer. When you come to the words _GO ON_ at the bottom of a page, continue working on the next page. When you come to the word _STOP_ at the bottom of page 37, put your pencils down. You may now begin.**

Allow students time to find and mark their answers.

9 Which numeral has a value between 7350 and 8430?

A 7160 C 7888

B 7229 D 8449

10 Which symbol would replace the ☐ in the following number sentence?

$$3 + 7 = 2 \;\square\; 5$$

J + L ×

K − M ÷

11 What would replace the ☐ to make the number sentence true?

$$(4 + 6) + 2 = (6 + \square) + 2$$

A 0 C 4

B 2 D 6

12 How could the following number sentence be solved?

$$8 + \square = 24$$

J Add 24 and 8.

K Multiply 24 times 8.

L Subtract 8 from 24.

M Divide 24 by 8.

13 Which numeral will make this number sentence true?

$$(4 \times \square) + 2 = 26$$

A 4 C 6

B 5 D 7

14 With his eyes closed, which card will Julio most likely pick from the following cards?

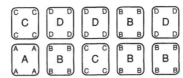

J A L C

K B M D

15 Which set of numbers shown here has the greatest average (mean)?

A {3, 4, 12}

B {4, 8, 2}

C {9, 7, 8}

D {5, 4, 13}

16 When Neil spins the spinner, on which number is the spinner most likely to stop?

J 1

K 2

L 3

M 4

17 A brown, a green, and a speckled lizard are in a box. **If the brown lizard is picked first, how many different ways can the other lizards be picked?**

A 1 C 3

B 2 D 4

GO ON

Answers

9 Ⓐ Ⓑ ● Ⓓ   11 Ⓐ Ⓑ ● Ⓓ   13 Ⓐ Ⓑ ● Ⓓ   15 Ⓐ Ⓑ ● Ⓓ   17 Ⓐ ● Ⓒ Ⓓ

10 Ⓙ Ⓚ ● Ⓜ   12 Ⓙ Ⓚ ● Ⓜ   14 Ⓙ ● Ⓛ Ⓜ   16 Ⓙ Ⓚ Ⓛ ●

18 The figure shown here has $\frac{3}{8}$ of its area shaded. How much is not shaded?

J $\frac{3}{5}$
K $\frac{5}{8}$
L $\frac{3}{11}$
M $\frac{5}{3}$

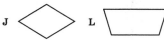

19 Which unit of measurement is best to use to describe the weight of a box of corn flakes?

A Feet
B Ounces
C Liters
D Inches

20 Which piece of material is the one cut from the fabric?

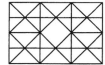

J

L

K

M

21 One yard is closest in value to which measurement?

A 1 kilogram
B 1 quart
C 1 liter
D 1 meter

22 Which figure is a parallelogram?

J

L

K

M

23 Which clock shows the time it will be in two and one-half hours, if it is 10:45 A.M. now?

A [1:15 P.M.]   C [1:30 P.M.]

B [1:45 P.M.]   D [2:15 P.M.]

24 Yolanda's herb garden is shaped like a rectangle. How many feet of fencing does she need to go around the entire garden?

8 ft.

22 ft.

J 16 feet
K 30 feet
L 60 feet
M 176 feet

GO ON

36

25 Which picture shows parallel lines?

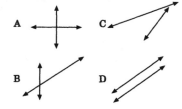

A · · · · · · ·

C

B

D

26 The closest estimate of 45,432 ÷ 9 is _____.

J 50   L 5000

K 500   M 50,000

27 The closest estimate of 4119 + 5915 _____.

A 4000 + 5000

B 4000 + 6000

C 5000 + 5000

D 5000 + 6000

28 The closest estimate of 348 ÷ 68 is _____.

J 3   L 5

K 4   M 6

29 The closest estimate of the cost of 44 juice boxes is _____.

1 juice box costs 29¢

A $0.15   C $12.00

B $0.70   D $28.00

30 The closest estimate of 650 ÷ 8 is _____.

J 8   L 800

K 80   M 8000

31 The closest estimate of the difference in the height of a California redwood tree and a Ponderosa pine tree is _____.

California redwood

Ponderosa pine

275 feet high   180 feet high

A 100 feet   C 300 feet

B 200 feet   D 400 feet

32 The closest estimate of 452 × 542 is _____.

J 400 × 500   L 500 × 600

K 500 × 500   M 400 × 600

33 The closest estimate of the number of gallons of gasoline needed is _____.

Car gets 27 miles per gallon.
Trip is 1,478 miles.

A 1400 ÷ 20   C 1500 ÷ 20

B 1400 ÷ 30   D 1500 ÷ 30

STOP

Level 11

Answers

25 Ⓐ Ⓑ Ⓒ ●   27 Ⓐ ● Ⓒ Ⓓ   29 Ⓐ Ⓑ ● Ⓓ   31 ● Ⓑ Ⓒ Ⓓ   33 Ⓐ Ⓑ Ⓒ ●
26 Ⓙ Ⓚ ● Ⓜ   28 Ⓙ Ⓚ ● Ⓜ   30 Ⓙ ● Ⓛ Ⓜ   32 Ⓙ ● Ⓛ Ⓜ

37

SAY: **It is now time to stop. You have completed the Unit 6 Test. Make sure that you have carefully filled in your answer spaces and have completely erased any stray marks. Then put your pencils down.**

After the test has been scored, review the questions and answer choices with students. If students are having difficulty with any lesson, provide them with additional practice items.

UNIT 7 — Math Problems

Lesson 15: Solving Problems

Directions: Darken the circle for the correct answer. Darken the circle for <u>Not given</u> if the answer is not shown.

> **TRY THIS**
> Read each problem carefully. Then decide how to find the correct answer.

S1 Renee's new bookcase has 4 shelves and will hold 168 books. Renee filled ¼ of it with books. **How many books did Renee put in the bookcase?**

A 21   C 56

B 42   D Not given

> **THINK IT THROUGH**
> The correct answer is B. To find how many books are on one shelf, divide the number of books by the number of shelves: 168 ÷ 4 = 42.

STOP

Read this story before working problems 1–4.

> Andy and Nate collect sports team pennants. Andy has 18 and Nate has 13. Ten of the pennants are duplicates.

1 How many more pennants does Andy have than Nate?

A 5   C 21

B 15   D Not given

2 Of the 18 pennants that Andy has, 4 are American League baseball and 6 are National League baseball. The rest are football pennants. **How many football pennants does he have?**

J 8   L 14

K 10   M Not given

3 How many different pennants do the boys have? (Do not count any team pennant more than once.)

A 9   C 21

B 15   D 31

4 The first pennants Nate bought one summer were American League baseball. Then he bought twice as many National League baseball pennants the next summer. **We would know how many baseball pennants he bought during these two summers if we knew**

J the number of American League pennants he bought during the second summer.

K the number of football pennants he owns.

L the total number of American League pennants he owns.

M the number of National League pennants he bought during the second summer.

5 Katie wants to make 42 baby bibs to sell at the craft fair next month. She has completed 14 of them. **How many bibs does she have left to make for the craft fair?**

A 28   C 56

B 30   D Not given

GO ON

Level 11

Answers

S1 Ⓐ ● Ⓒ Ⓓ   2 ● Ⓚ Ⓛ Ⓜ   4 Ⓙ Ⓚ Ⓛ ●

38   1 ● Ⓑ Ⓒ Ⓓ   3 Ⓐ Ⓑ ● Ⓓ   5 ● Ⓑ Ⓒ Ⓓ

UNIT 7: Math Problems

Lesson 15: Solving Problems

Mathematics Skills: Solving one-step and multiple-step word problems

Distribute scratch paper to students. Tell them to compute their answers on the scratch paper.

SAY: **Turn to Lesson 15, Solving Problems, on page 38.**

Check to see that all students find Lesson 15.

SAY: **In Lesson 15 you will practice solving word problems.**

Read the <u>Directions</u> to students.

SAY: **Now look at <u>Try This</u>.**

Read <u>Try This</u> to students.

SAY: **Now look at S1. Read the problem carefully. Decide how to find the correct answer. Work the problem, then darken the circle for the correct answer. Darken the circle for *Not given* if the correct answer is not given.**

Allow students time to find and mark their answer.

SAY: **Now look at <u>Think It Through</u>.**

Read <u>Think It Through</u> to students. Check to see that all students have filled in the correct answer space. Ask students if they have any questions.

SAY: **Now you will practice solving more word problems. Do numbers 1 through 11 just as we did S1. When you go to the words *GO ON* at the bottom of page 38, continue working on the next page. When you come to the word *STOP* at the bottom of page 39, put your pencils down. You may now begin.**

Allow students time to find and mark their answers.

China Gate Restaurant

Appetizers

Egg Roll	$1.20
Fried Won Ton (6)	$1.25
Shrimp Toast (2)	$2.75
B-B-Q Spareribs (4)	$4.95

Fried Rice

Pork, Chicken, or Beef	$4.95
Shrimp	$5.50
Combo (Chicken, Beef, Shrimp)	$5.75

House Specialities

Chicken

Chicken with Snow Peas	$7.50
Cashew Chicken	$7.50
Lemon Chicken	$6.75
Almond Chicken	$6.95
Spicy Chicken and Vegetables	$7.75

Beef

Beef with Broccoli	$8.25
Hot Spiced Shredded Beef	$8.25
Beef with Snow Peas	$8.25
Beef with Mushrooms	$8.50
Spicy Beef and Vegetables	$8.25

Pork

Sweet and Sour Pork	$6.95
Shredded Pork	$7.95
Spicy Pork and Vegetables	$7.25

Vegetables

Hot Spiced Bean Curd with Vegetables	$6.25
Spicy Mixed Vegetables	$5.95
Mixed Vegetable Saute	$5.95

Chop Suey, Chow Mein

Pork, Beef, or Chicken	$6.55
Shrimp	$6.95
Vegetable	$5.95
Combination	$6.95

Beverages

Chinese Tea	$0.80
Coffee	$0.80
Iced Tea	$0.90
Soft Drink	$0.90

For questions 6–11, use the restaurant menu shown here. Do not add sales tax.

6 How much did Lena pay for an egg roll, an order of shrimp fried rice, and a soft drink?

J $6.55   L $7.90

K $7.60   M Not given

7 Mr. Shen ordered beef with broccoli and his wife ordered spicy mixed vegetables. How much more did Mr. Shen pay for his dinner than for his wife's dinner?

A $.95   C $2.20

B $1.80   D Not given

8 Dee Ann and Wendy shared an order of fried won ton and an order of spareribs. Each ordered a soft drink and they split the bill evenly. How much did they each pay?

J $3.35   L $4.00

K $3.60   M Not given

9 Dora had a coupon for 20% off any order. She ordered an egg roll, cashew chicken, and iced tea. How much did she save by using the coupon?

A $1.27   C $1.92

B $1.58   D Not given

10 Mrs. Kimball and her two children each ordered combo fried rice and iced tea. What was Mrs. Kimball's total bill?

J $18.80   L $21.35

K $19.95   M Not given

11 Bernard ordered shrimp toast, combination chop suey, and coffee. What was Bernard's total bill?

A $9.10   C $11.90

B $10.40   D Not given

STOP

Level 11

Answers

6 ⓙ ● Ⓛ Ⓜ   8 ⓙ Ⓚ ● Ⓜ   10 ⓙ ● Ⓛ Ⓜ

7 Ⓐ Ⓑ Ⓒ ●   9 Ⓐ Ⓑ ● Ⓓ   11 Ⓐ Ⓑ Ⓒ ●

39

Lesson 16: Working with Graphs

Directions: Darken the circle for the correct answer.

TRY THIS Study the graph carefully. Look for key words or numbers in the question that tell you what to look for in the graph.

S1

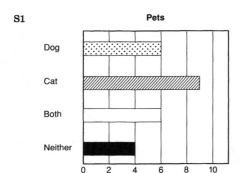

Pets

Dog

Cat

Both

Neither

0   2   4   6   8   10

Number of Students

This graph shows how many students have a dog, cat, both, or neither. **How many students have only a cat as a pet?**

A   4 students

B   6 students

C   9 students

D   14 students

THINK IT THROUGH The correct answer is C. There are 9 students who have only a cat as a pet, 6 students who have only a dog, 6 students with a dog and a cat, and 4 students who do not have a dog or a cat as a pet.

STOP

Use the graph to answer questions 1–3.

Favorite Warm-Weather Activity of Students	
Tennis	☼ ☼ ◗
Swimming	☼ ☼ ☼ ☼
Golfing	☼ ◗
Biking	☼ ☼ ☼ ◗
Hiking	☼ ☼ ☼

Each stands for 10.

1   How many students selected golf as their favorite activity?

A   15   C   30
B   25   D   35

2   How many students like biking and tennis?

J   25   L   60
K   35   K   70

3   About twice as many students prefer hiking to

A   golfing.
B   tennis.
C   swimming.
D   biking.

STOP

Level 11

40

Answers
S1 Ⓐ Ⓑ ● Ⓓ   2 Ⓙ Ⓚ ● Ⓜ
1 ● Ⓑ Ⓒ Ⓓ   3 ● Ⓑ Ⓒ Ⓓ

Lesson 16: Working with Graphs

Mathematics Skills: Analyzing graphs; evaluating graphic displays and using the information to solve problems

SAY: **Turn to Lesson 16, Working with Graphs, on page 40.**

Check to see that all students find Lesson 16.

SAY: **In Lesson 16 you will practice analyzing graphs and using the information to solve problems.**

Read the Directions to students.

SAY: **Now look at Try This.**

Read Try This to students.

SAY: **Now look at S1. Read the problem and study the graph carefully. Then darken the circle for the correct answer.**

Allow students time to find and mark their answer.

SAY: **Now look at Think It Through.**

Read Think It Through to students. Check to see that all students have filled in the correct answer space. Ask students if they have any questions.

SAY: **Now you will practice analyzing more graphs. Do numbers 1 through 3 just as we did S1. When you come to the word STOP at the bottom of page 40, put your pencils down. You may now begin.**

Allow students time to find and mark their answers.

Review the questions and answer choices with students. Discuss with the class why one answer is correct and the others are not correct. Also check to see that students have carefully filled in the answer spaces and have completely erased any stray marks.

S1 The records at the public library show that 3,782 books were borrowed during March. Only 2,165 books were borrowed during December. **How many more books were borrowed during March than during December?**

A 1,617   C 5,947

B 1,623   D Not given

STOP

For questions 1–12, darken the circle for the correct answer. Darken the circle for <u>Not given</u> if the answer is not shown.

Use the menu below to answer questions 1-6.

MENU	
Hamburger	$1.40
Hot dog	$1.00
Fruit	$0.50
Yogurt	$0.60
Pizza slice	$1.25
Cookies	$0.75
Chips	$0.40
Milk	$0.50
Fries	$0.75
Juice	$0.50
Salad	$1.00
Soda	$0.60

1 How much did Theresa pay for a hot dog, yogurt, and juice?

A $2.00   C $2.25

B $2.10   D Not given

2 Mrs. Delgado bought a hamburger for herself and 2 pizza slices for Matt. **How much more did Mrs. Delgado pay for Matt's pizza than her own sandwich?**

J $0.15   L $1.10

K $1.00   M Not given

3 Todd and Akio shared four hot dogs, an order of fries, and a bag of cookies. **How much did they each pay?**

A $2.25   C $2.75

B $2.50   D Not given

4 Today's special is a hamburger, chips, and juice for $2.00. **How much will Emily save if she buys the special instead of the separate items?**

J $0.20   L $0.30

K $0.25   M Not given

5 Mr. and Mrs. Gossett and their 2 children each ordered a pizza slice and a soda. **How much did they pay altogether?**

A $6.40   C $7.50

B $7.40   D Not given

6 Marty bought 2 hot dogs, 2 hamburgers, 2 chips, and 2 fries. **He spent the same amount of money as if he had bought**

J 4 pizza slices, 3 juices, and 1 soda.

K 4 hamburgers, 2 salads, and 4 milks.

L 3 salads, 2 yogurts, and 5 juices.

M 5 hot dogs and 4 fries.

GO ON

Level 11

Answers
S1 ● Ⓑ Ⓒ Ⓓ   2 Ⓙ Ⓚ ● Ⓜ   4 Ⓙ Ⓚ ● Ⓜ   6 ● Ⓚ Ⓛ Ⓜ
1 Ⓐ ● Ⓒ Ⓓ   3 Ⓐ Ⓑ ● Ⓓ   5 Ⓐ ● Ⓒ Ⓓ

41

Unit 7 Test

Distribute scratch paper to students. Tell them to compute their answers on the scratch paper.

SAY: **Turn to the Unit 7 Test on page 41.**

Check to see that all students find the Unit 7 Test.

SAY: **In this test you will use the mathematics skills that we have practiced in this unit. We will work the sample together before you begin the test. Look at S1. Read the problem carefully. Yo are asked to find how many more books were borrowed durin March than during December. Darken the circle for the correc answer.**

Allow students time to find and mark their answer.

SAY: **You should have darkened the circle for *A*. You should subtract 2,165—the number of books borrowed during December, from 3,782—the number of books borrowed durin March. The answer is *1,617*.**

Check to see that all students have filled in the correct answer space. Ask students if they have any questions.

SAY: **Now you will finish the test on your own. Do numbers 1 through 12 just as we did the sample. Read the questions an answer choices carefully. Then darken the circle for each correct answer. When you come to the words *GO ON* at the bottom of page 41, continue working on the next page. When you come to the word *STOP* at the bottom of page 42, put you pencils down. You may now begin.**

Allow students time to find and mark their answers.

The graph below shows the source of each $100 collected by the PTA. Use the graph to answer questions 7–9.

PTA Income Sources

The following graph shows how many hours Lisa baby-sat last week. Use the graph to answer questions 10–12.

Lisa's Baby-sitting Record

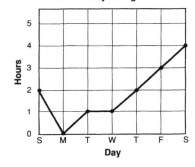

7 **How much of each $100 comes from Market Day?**

A $10

B $16

C $24

D $41

8 **Which of these income sources is more than twice the book fair income?**

J Market Day

K Fall fiesta

L Pizza lunches

M Spring plant sale

9 **Which two sources are about the same amount?**

A Fall fiesta and Market Day

B Spring plant sale and pizza lunches

C Book fair and spring plant sale

D Book fair and Market Day

10 **On which day did Lisa baby-sit for 3 hours?**

J Thursday

K Friday

L Saturday

M Sunday

11 **Lisa did not baby-sit on**

A Monday.

B Tuesday.

C Wednesday.

D Saturday.

12 **Which best describes Lisa's time spent baby-sitting between Wednesday and Saturday?**

J It decreased each day.

K It increased each day.

L It showed no change.

M It decreased and then increased each day.

STOP

Level 11

Answers

7 Ⓐ Ⓑ ● Ⓓ   9 Ⓐ ● Ⓒ Ⓓ   11 ● Ⓑ Ⓒ Ⓓ

8 Ⓙ ● Ⓛ Ⓜ   10 Ⓙ ● Ⓛ Ⓜ   12 Ⓙ ● Ⓛ Ⓜ

42

SAY: **It is now time to stop. You have completed the Unit 7 Test. Make sure that you have carefully filled in your answer spaces and have completely erased any stray marks. Then put your pencils down.**

After the test has been scored, review the questions and answer choices with students. If students are having difficulty with any lesson, provide them with additional practice items.

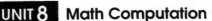

─── Lesson 17: Adding ───

Directions: Darken the circle for the correct answer. Darken the circle for <u>N</u> if the answer is <u>not</u> given.

TRY THIS	Add each column of digits. Remember to regroup when necessary, and align any decimals. Write the sum, and check it against the answer choices.

S1

$138 + 46 =$

A 174
B 184
C 598
D N

THINK IT THROUGH	The correct answer is B. First, rewrite the addends so that the ones and tens are aligned.

Then, add the ones digits, 8 + 6 = 14.
Regroup 14 ones as 1 ten and 4 ones.
Next, add the tens digits, 1 + 3 + 4 = 8 tens.
Finally, add the hundreds digits, 1 + 0 = 1.

STOP

Reduce answers that are fractions to lowest terms.

1
$4000 + 46 =$

A 4046
B 4460
C 46,400
D N

4
$6.17 + 7.96 =$

J 14.13
K 141.3
L 1413
M N

2

$\frac{6}{12} + \frac{1}{12} + \frac{4}{12} =$

J $\frac{11}{12}$
K $\frac{11}{36}$
L $\frac{24}{12}$
M N

5
$6 + 137 + 89 =$

A 212
B 222
C 232
D N

3

$\frac{5}{8}$
$+ \frac{1}{8}$

A $\frac{6}{12}$
B $\frac{2}{3}$
C 1
D N

6

1648
+ 267

J 1805
K 1915
L 1925
M N

STOP

Level 11

Answers
S1 Ⓐ ● Ⓒ Ⓓ   2 ● Ⓚ Ⓛ Ⓜ   4 ● Ⓚ Ⓛ Ⓜ   6 Ⓙ ● Ⓛ Ⓜ
1 ● Ⓑ Ⓒ Ⓓ   3 Ⓐ Ⓑ ● Ⓓ   5 Ⓐ Ⓑ ● Ⓓ

43

UNIT 8 Math Computation

Lesson 17: Adding

Mathematics Skills: Adding whole numbers, decimals, fractions, and mixed numbers

Distribute scratch paper to students. Tell them to compute their answers on the scratch paper.

SAY: **Turn to Lesson 17, Adding, on page 43.**

Check to see that all students find Lesson 17.

SAY: **In Lesson 17 you will practice adding whole numbers, decimals, fractions, and mixed numbers.**

Read the <u>Directions</u> to students.

SAY: **Now look at <u>Try This</u>.**

Read <u>Try This</u> to students.

SAY: **Now look at S1. You are asked to add 138 and 46. Work the problem, then darken the circle for the correct answer. If the correct answer is not given, darken the circle for _N_.**

Allow students time to find and mark their answer.

SAY: **Now look at <u>Think It Through</u>.**

Read <u>Think It Through</u> to students. Check to see that all students have filled in the correct answer space. Remind students to reduce answers that are fractions to lowest terms. Ask students if they have any question

SAY: **Now you will practice solving more addition problems. Do numbers 1 through 6 just as we did S1. When you come to the word _STOP_ at the bottom of page 43, put your pencils down. You may now begin.**

Allow students time to find and mark their answers.

Review the questions and answer choices with students. Discuss with the class why one answer is correct and the others are not correct. Also che to see that students have carefully filled in the answer spaces and have completely erased any stray marks.

Lesson 18: Subtracting

Directions: Darken the circle for the correct answer. Darken the circle for <u>N</u> if the answer is <u>not</u> given.

TRY
THIS
Remember to regroup when necessary. **Check your answer by covering the top number and adding the answer and the second number. The covered number and the sum should be equal.**

S1
800
− 16

A 784
B 785
C 816
D N

THINK IT THROUGH The correct answer is A. It is necessary to regroup The 800 as 7 hundreds, 9 tens, and 10 ones. Check the answer by adding 16 and 784.

STOP

Reduce answers that are fractions to lowest terms.

1 6247 − 34 =

A 6113
B 6213
C 6281
D N

2
365
− 68

J 203
K 207
L 297
M N

3
571
− 264

A 307
B 316
C 835
D N

4 2943 − 1600 =

J 1243
K 1343
L 1443
M N

5 0.21 − 0.07 =

A 0.14
B 0.28
C 21.07
D N

6
$\frac{16}{18}$
− $\frac{3}{18}$

J $\frac{3}{4}$
K 1$\frac{1}{8}$
L 12
M N

7 $\frac{11}{8}$ − $\frac{5}{8}$ =

A $\frac{6}{16}$
B $\frac{3}{4}$
C 2
D N

8 8.3 − 4.5 =

J 3.8
K 4.2
L 4.8
M N

STOP

Level 11

Answers
S1 ● Ⓑ Ⓒ Ⓓ   2 Ⓙ Ⓚ ● Ⓜ   4 Ⓙ ● Ⓛ Ⓜ   6 ● Ⓚ Ⓛ Ⓜ   8 ● Ⓚ Ⓛ Ⓜ
44
1 Ⓐ ● Ⓒ Ⓓ   3 Ⓑ Ⓒ Ⓓ   5 ● Ⓑ Ⓒ Ⓓ   7 Ⓐ ● Ⓒ Ⓓ

Lesson 18: Subtracting

Mathematics Skills: Subtracting whole numbers, decimals, fractions, and mixed numbers

Distribute scratch paper to students. Tell them to compute their answers on the scratch paper.

SAY: **Turn to Lesson 18, Subtracting, on page 44.**

Check to see that all students find Lesson 18.

SAY: **In Lesson 18 you will practice subtracting whole numbers, decimals, fractions, and mixed numbers.**

Read the <u>Directions</u> to students.

SAY: **Now look at <u>Try This</u>.**

Read <u>Try This</u> to students.

SAY: **Now look at S1. You are asked to subtract 16 from 800. Work the problem, then darken the circle for the correct answer. If the correct answer is not given, darken the circle for _N_.**

Allow students time to find and mark their answer.

SAY: **Now look at <u>Think It Through</u>.**

Read <u>Think It Through</u> to students. Check to see that all students have filled in the correct answer space. Remind students to reduce answers that are fractions to lowest terms. Ask students if they have any questions.

SAY: **Now you will practice solving more subtraction problems. Do numbers 1 through 8 just as we did S1. When you come to the word _STOP_ at the bottom of page 44, put your pencils down. You may now begin.**

Allow students time to find and mark their answers.

Review the questions and answer choices with students. Discuss with the class why one answer is correct and the others are not correct. Also check to see that students have carefully filled in the answer spaces and have completely erased any stray marks.

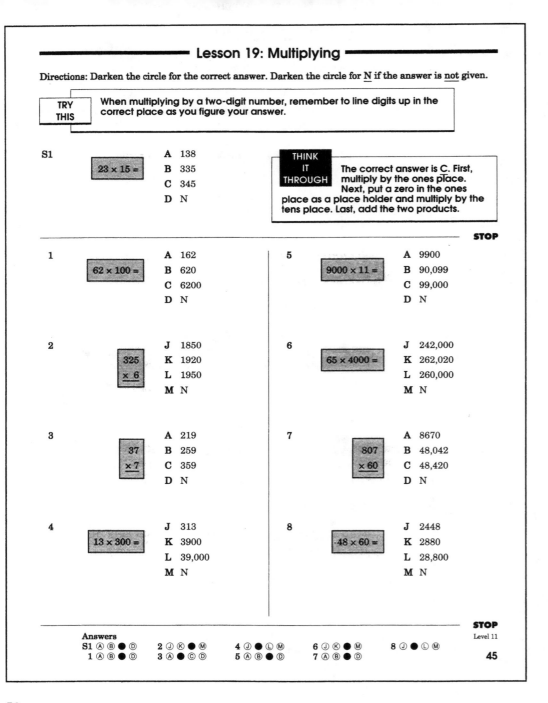

Lesson 19: Multiplying

Mathematics Skill: Multiplying whole numbers

Distribute scratch paper to students. Tell them to compute their answers on the scratch paper.

SAY: **Turn to Lesson 19, Multiplying, on page 45.**

Check to see that all students find Lesson 19.

SAY: **In Lesson 19 you will practice multiplying whole numbers.**

Read the Directions to students.

SAY: **Now look at Try This.**

Read Try This to students.

SAY: **Now look at S1. You are asked to multiply 23 by 15. Work the problem, then darken the circle for the correct answer. If the correct answer is not given, darken the circle for N.**

Allow students time to find and mark their answer.

SAY: **Now look at Think It Through.**

Read Think It Through to students. Check to see that all students have filled in the correct answer space. Ask students if they have any questions.

SAY: **Now you will practice solving more multiplication problems. Do numbers 1 through 8 just as we did S1. When you come to the word *STOP* at the bottom of page 45, put your pencils down. You may now begin.**

Allow students time to find and mark their answers.

Review the questions and answer choices with students. Discuss with the class why one answer is correct and the others are not correct. Also check to see that students have carefully filled in the answer spaces and have completely erased any stray marks.

Lesson 20: Dividing

Directions: Darken the circle for the correct answer. Darken the circle for <u>N</u> if the answer is <u>not</u> given.

TRY THIS — Check the answer to a division problem by multiplying the answer by the divisor in the problem. Then add any remainder. The result should equal the dividend.

S1
- A 150 r2
- B 152
- C 152 r2
- D N

THINK IT THROUGH — The correct answer is C. Check this by multiplying 152 x 4 to get 608. Then, add the remainder 2 to get 610.

STOP

1 307 ÷ 8 =
- A 38
- B 38 r3
- C 308 r3
- D N

5 8)428
- A 51
- B 53
- C 53 r4
- D N

2 6)4506
- J 701
- K 751
- L 851
- M N

6 4)7084
- J 1011
- K 1071
- L 1771
- M N

3 130 ÷ 5 =
- A 16
- B 26
- C 650
- D N

7 83 ÷ 4 =
- A 20
- B 20 r3
- C 23
- D N

4 864 ÷ 2 =
- J 234
- K 430
- L 432
- M N

8 45 ÷ 3 =
- J 15
- K 42
- L 48
- M N

STOP

Level 11

Answers
S1 Ⓐ Ⓑ ● Ⓓ   2 Ⓙ ● Ⓛ Ⓜ   4 Ⓙ Ⓚ ● Ⓜ   6 Ⓙ Ⓚ ● Ⓜ   8 ● Ⓚ Ⓛ Ⓜ
46   1 Ⓐ ● Ⓒ Ⓓ   3 Ⓐ ● Ⓒ Ⓓ   5 Ⓐ Ⓑ ● Ⓓ   7 Ⓐ ● Ⓒ Ⓓ

Lesson 20: Dividing

Mathematics Skill: Dividing whole numbers

Distribute scratch paper to students. Tell them to compute their answers on the scratch paper.

SAY: **Turn to Lesson 20, Dividing, on page 46.**

Check to see that all students find Lesson 20.

SAY: **In Lesson 20 you will practice dividing whole numbers.**

Read the <u>Directions</u> to students.

SAY: **Now look at <u>Try This</u>.**

Read <u>Try This</u> to students.

SAY: **Now look at S1. You are asked to divide 610 by 4. Work the problem, then darken the circle for the correct answer. If the correct answer is not given, darken the circle for N.**

Allow students time to find and mark their answer.

SAY: **Now look at <u>Think It Through</u>.**

Read <u>Think It Through</u> to students. Check to see that all students have filled in the correct answer space. Ask students if they have any questions.

SAY: **Now you will practice solving more division problems. Do numbers 1 through 8 just as we did S1. When you come to the word *STOP* at the bottom of page 46, put your pencils down. You may now begin.**

Allow students time to find and mark their answers.

Review the questions and answer choices with students. Discuss with the class why one answer is correct and the others are not correct. Also check to see that students have carefully filled in the answer spaces and have completely erased any stray marks.

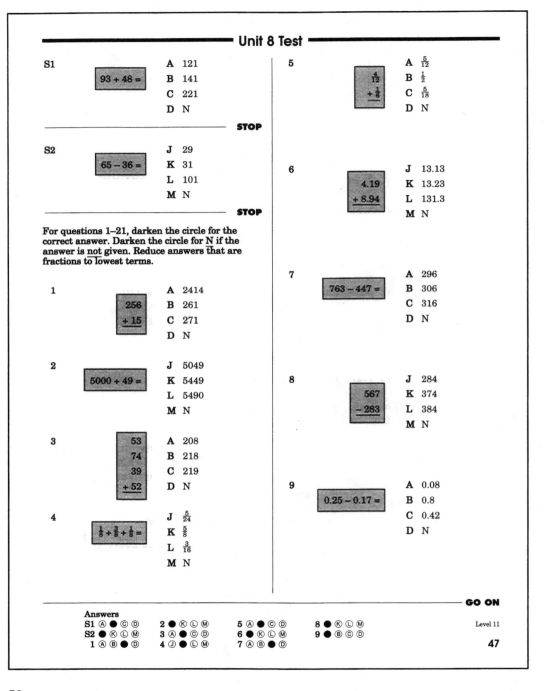

Unit 8 Test

S1 $93 + 48 =$
- A 121
- B 141
- C 221
- D N

STOP

S2 $65 - 36 =$
- J 29
- K 31
- L 101
- M N

STOP

For questions 1–21, darken the circle for the correct answer. Darken the circle for N if the answer is not given. Reduce answers that are fractions to lowest terms.

1 256 + 15
- A 2414
- B 261
- C 271
- D N

2 $5000 + 49 =$
- J 5049
- K 5449
- L 5490
- M N

3 53 74 39 + 52
- A 208
- B 218
- C 219
- D N

4 $\frac{1}{2} + \frac{2}{8} + \frac{1}{8} =$
- J $\frac{5}{24}$
- K $\frac{5}{8}$
- L $\frac{3}{16}$
- M N

5 $\frac{4}{12} + \frac{1}{8}$
- A $\frac{5}{12}$
- B $\frac{1}{2}$
- C $\frac{5}{18}$
- D N

6 4.19 + 8.94
- J 13.13
- K 13.23
- L 131.3
- M N

7 $763 - 447 =$
- A 296
- B 306
- C 316
- D N

8 567 − 283
- J 284
- K 374
- L 384
- M N

9 $0.25 - 0.17 =$
- A 0.08
- B 0.8
- C 0.42
- D N

GO ON

Answers
S1 Ⓐ ● Ⓒ Ⓓ   2 ● Ⓚ Ⓛ Ⓜ   5 Ⓐ ● Ⓒ Ⓓ   8 ● Ⓚ Ⓛ Ⓜ   Level 11
S2 ● Ⓚ Ⓛ Ⓜ   3 Ⓐ ● Ⓒ Ⓓ   6 ● Ⓚ Ⓛ Ⓜ   9 ● Ⓑ Ⓒ Ⓓ   **47**
1 Ⓐ Ⓑ ● Ⓓ   4 Ⓙ ● Ⓛ Ⓜ   7 Ⓐ Ⓑ ● Ⓓ

Unit 8 Test

Distribute scratch paper to students. Tell them to compute their answers on the scratch paper.

SAY: **Turn to the Unit 8 Test on page 47.**

Check to see that all students find the Unit 8 Test.

SAY: **In this test you will use the mathematics skills that we have practiced in this unit. Look at S1. You are asked to add 93 and 48. Darken the circle for the correct answer.**

Allow students time to find and mark their answer.

SAY: **You should have darkened the circle for B because 93 + 48 = 141.**

Check to see that all students have filled in the correct answer space. Ask students if they have any questions.

SAY: **Now look at S2. You are asked to subtract 36 from 65. Darken the circle for the correct answer.**

Allow students time to find and mark their answer.

SAY: **You should have darkened the circle for J because 65 − 36 = 29.**

Check to see that all students have filled in the correct answer space. Ask students if they have any questions.

SAY: **Now you will finish the test on your own. Do numbers 1 through 21 just as we did the samples. Read the problems and answer choices carefully. Then darken the circle for each correct answer. When you come to the words GO ON at the bottom of a page, continue working on the next page. When you come to the word STOP at the bottom of page 48, put your pencils down. You may now begin.**

Allow students time to find and mark their answers.

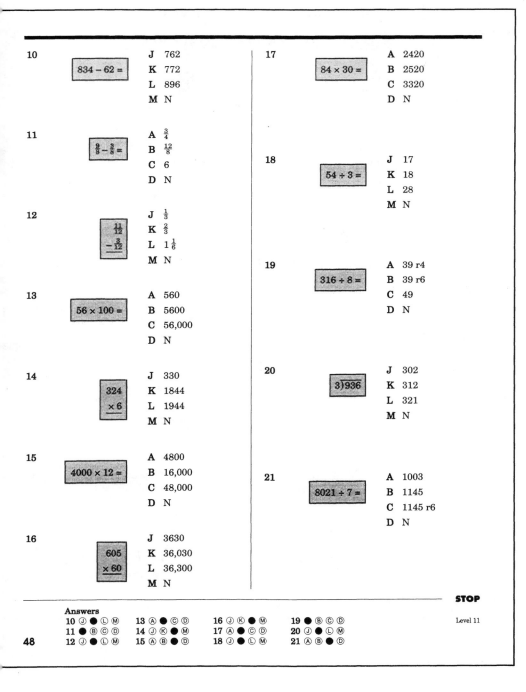

10　834 − 62 =　　J　762
　　　　　　　　　K　772
　　　　　　　　　L　896
　　　　　　　　　M　N

11　$\frac{9}{8} - \frac{3}{8} =$　A　$\frac{3}{4}$
　　　　　　　　　B　$\frac{12}{8}$
　　　　　　　　　C　6
　　　　　　　　　D　N

12　$\frac{11}{12}$
　　$-\frac{3}{12}$　J　$\frac{1}{3}$
　　　　　　　　　K　$\frac{2}{3}$
　　　　　　　　　L　$1\frac{1}{6}$
　　　　　　　　　M　N

13　56 × 100 =　　A　560
　　　　　　　　　B　5600
　　　　　　　　　C　56,000
　　　　　　　　　D　N

14　324
　　× 6　　　　　J　330
　　　　　　　　　K　1844
　　　　　　　　　L　1944
　　　　　　　　　M　N

15　4000 × 12 =　A　4800
　　　　　　　　　B　16,000
　　　　　　　　　C　48,000
　　　　　　　　　D　N

16　605
　　× 60　　　　J　3630
　　　　　　　　　K　36,030
　　　　　　　　　L　36,300
　　　　　　　　　M　N

17　84 × 30 =　　A　2420
　　　　　　　　　B　2520
　　　　　　　　　C　3320
　　　　　　　　　D　N

18　54 ÷ 3 =　　J　17
　　　　　　　　　K　18
　　　　　　　　　L　28
　　　　　　　　　M　N

19　316 ÷ 8 =　　A　39 r4
　　　　　　　　　B　39 r6
　　　　　　　　　C　49
　　　　　　　　　D　N

20　3)936　　　　J　302
　　　　　　　　　K　312
　　　　　　　　　L　321
　　　　　　　　　M　N

21　8021 ÷ 7 =　A　1003
　　　　　　　　　B　1145
　　　　　　　　　C　1145 r6
　　　　　　　　　D　N

STOP

SAY:　**It is now time to stop. You have completed the Unit 8 Test. Make sure that you have carefully filled in your answer spaces and have completely erased any stray marks. Then put your pencils down.**

After the test has been scored, review the questions and answer choices with students. If students are having difficulty, provide them with additional practice.

Answers
10 Ⓙ ● Ⓛ Ⓜ　13 Ⓐ ● Ⓒ Ⓓ　16 Ⓙ Ⓚ ● Ⓜ　19 ● Ⓑ Ⓒ Ⓓ
11 ● Ⓑ Ⓒ Ⓓ　14 Ⓙ Ⓚ ● Ⓜ　17 Ⓐ ● Ⓒ Ⓓ　20 Ⓙ ● Ⓛ Ⓜ
12 Ⓙ ● Ⓛ Ⓜ　15 Ⓐ Ⓑ ● Ⓓ　18 Ⓙ ● Ⓛ Ⓜ　21 Ⓐ Ⓑ ● Ⓓ

Level 11

48

UNIT 9 Maps and Diagrams

Lesson 21: Working with Maps

Directions: Darken the circle for the correct answer.

TRY THIS	The map is of an imaginary country made up of four states. The map shows the resources and products of the country. The map also includes a key and a compass rose. Study the information shown in the map.

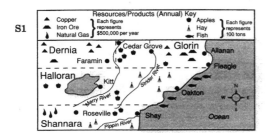

S1

About how much hay is produced in Shannara each year?

A 100 tons

B 300 tons

C 600 tons

D 1,500 tons

THINK IT THROUGH	The correct answer is B. The map key states that each hay symbol represents 100 tons. Since there are three hay symbols shown in Shannara, there are 300 tons of hay produced there each year.

STOP

Use the map in S1 to answer questions 1–4.

1 In what city is fishing probably an important part of the economy?

A Shay   C Kitt

B Oakton   D Allanan

2 What is the value of iron ore produced in Glorin each year?

J $500,000

K $1,000,000

L $1,500,000

M $2,000,000

3 In addition to hay and apples, what else is produced in Shannara?

A Copper

B Iron ore

C Fish

D Natural gas

4 If you went from Shannara to Cedar Grove on the Strider River, in which direction would you be traveling?

J Northwest   L Southwest

K Northeast   M Southeast

GO ON

Answers
S1 Ⓐ ● Ⓒ Ⓓ   2 Ⓙ Ⓚ ● Ⓜ   4 Ⓙ ● Ⓛ Ⓜ
1 Ⓐ ● Ⓒ Ⓓ   3 Ⓐ Ⓑ Ⓒ ●

UNIT 9 Maps and Diagrams

Lesson 21: Working with Maps

Study Skills: Using map symbols and keys to describe and locate places determining direction and distance; interpreting data on population, transportation, production, elevation, and resources; tracing travel routes

SAY: **Turn to Lesson 21, Working with Maps, page 49.**

Check to see that all students find Lesson 21.

SAY: **In Lesson 21 you will practice using maps to answer questions.**

Read the Directions to students.

SAY: **Now look at Try This.**

Read Try This to students.

SAY: **Now look at S1. Study the map and key to see what the symbols mean and where they are located. Study the compass rose to find directions.** (Allow one minute for students to study the map.) **Now read the question and answer choices carefully. Then darken the circle for the choice that shows ho much hay is produced in Shannara each year.**

Allow students time to find and mark their answer.

SAY: **Now look at Think It Through.**

Read Think It Through to students. Check to see that students have fille in the correct answer space. Ask students if they have any questions.

SAY: **Now you will practice using maps to answer more questions. Do numbers 1 through 11 just as we did S1. When you come t the words GO ON at the bottom of page 49, continue working on the next page. When you come to the word STOP at the bottom of page 50, put your pencils down. You may now begi**

Allow students time to find and mark their answers.

Review the questions and answer choices with students. Discuss with the class why one answer is correct and the others are not correct. Also check to see that students have carefully filled in the answer spaces and have completely erased any stray marks.

Use the map shown here to answer questions 5–11.

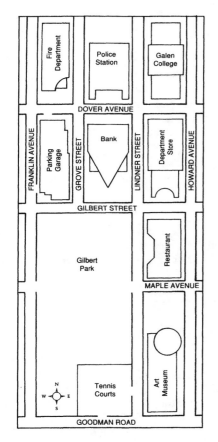

5 Which direction is the parking garage from the department store?

A North   C East

B South   D West

6 Which direction is Galen College from the art museum?

J North   L East

K South   M West

7 People can enter the tennis courts in Gilbert Park from

A Lindner and Maple.

B Lindner and Goodman.

C Lindner and Gilbert.

D Maple and Gilbert.

8 Which is located on the south side of Dover Avenue?

J The restaurant

K The police station

L The bank

M The fire department

9 To go from the fire department to the restaurant, Jenna walked

A east, then south.

B west, then south.

C east, then north.

D west, then north.

10 Which is closest to the art museum?

J The department store

K The bank

L Gilbert Park

M Galen College

11 Which route did Ann use to go from the bank to the tennis courts?

A Grove, then Dover

B Dover, then Maple

C Gilbert, then Lindner

D Gilbert, then Howard

STOP

Level 11

Directions: Darken the circle for the correct answer.

TRY THIS	Before you select your answer, carefully read all the information given in the schedule.

S1

County Fair Events				
	11:00 12:00	1:00	2:00	3:00
FRI.	Judging of 4-H craft projects	Footraces — — — — — —→		
		Toddlers	4–5 year olds	6–8 year olds
SAT.	Pet parade	Footraces — — — — — —→		
	Judging of 4-H farming projects	9–10 year olds	11–12 year olds	13–14 year olds
			Teddy bear picnic	
SUN.	Baby contest	Crowning of 4-H king and queen	Marching band contest	
	Judging of 4-H livestock projects			

How many events are scheduled for Sunday?

A 2

B 4

C 6

D 7

THINK IT THROUGH	The correct answer is B. There are four events scheduled for Sunday: a baby contest, judging of livestock projects, crowning the king and queen, and a marching band contest.

STOP

Use the table in S1 to answer questions 1–4.

1 If eleven-year-old Carole and twelve-year-old Rachel entered the footraces, when would their race begin?

A Friday at 1:00 P.M.

B Friday at 3:00 P.M.

C Saturday at 1:00 P.M.

D Saturday at 2:00 P.M.

2 When is the marching band contest scheduled to take place?

J Sunday at 11:00 A.M.

K Saturday at 2:00 P.M.

L Sunday at 2:00 P.M.

M Saturday at 11:00 A.M.

3 How many events are scheduled for Saturday?

A 2

B 4

C 6

D 7

4 For a 4-H project, Kyle raised a pig named Rufus and entered him in the fair. When would Kyle learn whether Rufus won a prize?

J By 11:00 A.M. Friday

K By 1:00 P.M. Friday

L By 2:00 P.M. Saturday

M By 1:00 P.M. Sunday

STOP

Level 11

Answers
S1 Ⓐ ● Ⓒ Ⓓ   2 Ⓙ Ⓚ ● Ⓜ   4 Ⓙ Ⓚ Ⓛ ●
1 Ⓐ Ⓑ Ⓒ ●   3 Ⓐ Ⓑ ● Ⓓ

51

Lesson 22: Working with Charts and Diagrams

Study Skills: Interpreting information in schedules, charts, tables, and diagrams

SAY: **Turn to Lesson 22, Working with Charts and Diagrams, page 51.**

Check to see that all students find Lesson 22.

SAY: **In Lesson 22 you will practice interpreting information presented in visual materials.**

Read the Directions to students.

SAY: **Now look at Try This.**

Read Try This to students.

SAY: **Now look at S1. Study the schedule. Read the question and answer choices carefully. Then darken the circle for the choice that shows the number of events that are scheduled for Sunday.**

Allow students time to find and mark their answer.

SAY: **Now look at Think It Through.**

Read Think It Through to students. Check to see that students have filled in the correct answer space. Ask students if they have any questions.

SAY: **Now you will use the schedule to answer more questions. Do numbers 1 through 4 just as we did S1. When you come to the word STOP at the bottom of page 51, put your pencils down. You may now begin.**

Allow students time to find and mark their answers.

Review the questions and answer choices with students. Discuss with the class why one answer is correct and the others are not correct. Also check to see that students have carefully filled in the answer spaces and have completely erased any stray marks.

Unit 9 Test

S1

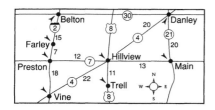

Which city has three highways running through it?

A Preston

B Trell

C Danley

D Main

STOP

For questions 1–18, darken the circle for the correct answer.

The maps show an imaginary country made up of four states. The top map shows major cities, rivers, and highways. The bottom map shows resources and products. Use these maps to answer questions 1–4.

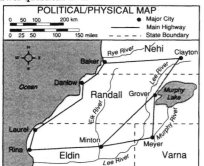

POLITICAL/PHYSICAL MAP

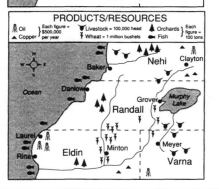

PRODUCTS/RESOURCES

1 If a boat sailed from Meyer to Murphy Lake on the Murphy River, in which direction would it travel?

A Southeast   C Northeast

B Southwest   D Northwest

2 Where is most of the wheat produced?

J Along the Rye River

K Near Grover

L Along the Elk River

M West of Grover

3 About how much fish is produced each year?

A About 200 tons

B About 400 tons

C About 1,000 tons

D About 10,000 tons

4 About how many miles is Rina from Minton?

J About 50 miles

K About 75 miles

L About 110 miles

M About 150 miles

GO ON

Level 11

Answers

S1 Ⓐ Ⓑ ● Ⓓ   2 Ⓙ Ⓚ ● Ⓜ   4 Ⓙ Ⓚ Ⓛ ●

52

1 Ⓐ Ⓑ ● Ⓓ   3 Ⓐ Ⓑ ● Ⓓ

Unit 9 Test

SAY: **Turn to the Unit 9 Test on page 52.**

Check to see that all students find the Unit 9 Test.

SAY: **In this test you will use the study skills that we have practiced in this unit. Look at S1. Study the map. You are asked to tell which city has three highways passing through it. Darken the circle for the correct answer.**

Allow students time to find and mark their answer.

SAY: **You should have darkened the circle for *C* because the map shows that highways 4, 21, and 30 pass through the city of *Danley*.**

Check to see that all students have filled in the correct answer space. Ask students if they have any questions.

SAY: **Now you will finish the test on your own. Do numbers 1 through 18 just as we did S1. Study the visual materials. Read the questions and answer choices carefully. Then darken the circle for each correct answer. When you come to the words *GO ON* at the bottom of a page, continue working on the next page. When you come to the word *STOP* at the bottom of page 54, put your pencils down. You may now begin.**

Allow students time to find and mark their answers.

Level 11   63

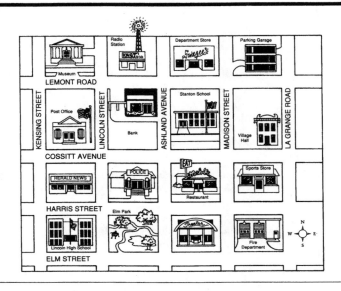

Use the map shown here, which shows part of a city, to answer questions 5–10.

5 Which is located on the south side of Cossitt Avenue?

A The post office

B The sports store

C The parking garage

D The theater

6 Which is located along Ashland Avenue?

J The post office

K The village hall

L The Herald News

M The restaurant

7 People can enter the museum from

A Lemont and Kensing.

B Kensing and Lincoln.

C Lemont and Lincoln.

D Lemont and Ashland.

8 To walk from the bank to the theater, a person would walk

J south, then east.

K south, then west.

L north, then east.

M north, then west.

9 The parking garage is closest to which building?

A The theater

B Lincoln High School

C The sports store

D The post office

10 Which direction is the bank from Elm Park?

J North   L East

K South   M West

GO ON

Level 11

Answers

5 Ⓐ ● Ⓒ Ⓓ   7 Ⓐ Ⓑ ● Ⓓ   9 Ⓐ Ⓑ ● Ⓓ

6 Ⓙ Ⓚ Ⓛ ●   8 ● Ⓚ Ⓛ Ⓜ   10 ● Ⓚ Ⓛ Ⓜ

53

Use the diagram shown here to answer questions 11–18.

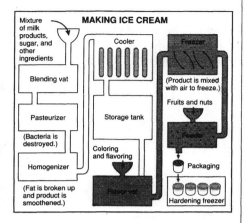

MAKING ICE CREAM

Mixture of milk products, sugar, and other ingredients

Blending vat

Cooler

Freezer

(Product is mixed with air to freeze.)

Fruits and nuts

Pasteurizer

(Bacteria is destroyed.)

Storage tank

Feeder

Homogenizer

Coloring and flavoring

(Fat is broken up and product is smoothened.)

Flavor vat

Packaging

Hardening freezer

11 What does the diagram show?

A How ice cream is served

B How ice cream is shipped to stores

C How ice cream flavors are taste-tested

D How ice cream is made

12 How many total steps are shown on the diagram, starting with mixing the ingredients?

J 6

K 8

L 10

M 11

13 Where is the fat in the product broken up and the product made smooth?

A In the homogenizer

B In the pasteurizer

C In the feeder

D In the blending vat

14 What happens to the ice cream after fruit and nuts have been added?

J It is frozen.

K It is pasteurized.

L It is homogenized.

M It is packaged.

15 Which are added to the ice cream mixture at the same step in the process?

A Milk and nuts

B Fruit and fat

C Coloring and flavoring

D Fruit and flavoring

16 What happens to the ice cream mixture in the pasteurizer?

J Flavoring is added.

K Bacteria is destroyed.

L Ingredients are blended.

M Ingredients are frozen.

17 What is mixed with the ice cream ingredients to freeze the mixture?

A Air

B Fruits and nuts

C Milk

D Flavoring

18 Where is coloring added to the mixture?

J In the freezer

K In the blending vat

L In the flavor vat

M In the feeder

STOP

Level 11

Answers
11 Ⓐ Ⓑ Ⓒ ●   13 ● Ⓑ Ⓒ Ⓓ   15 Ⓐ Ⓑ ● Ⓓ   17 ● Ⓑ Ⓒ Ⓓ
54 12 Ⓙ Ⓚ ● Ⓜ   14 Ⓙ Ⓚ Ⓛ ●   16 Ⓙ ● Ⓛ Ⓜ   18 Ⓙ Ⓚ ● Ⓜ

SAY: **It is now time to stop. You have completed the Unit 9 Test. Make sure that you have carefully filled in your answer spaces and have completely erased any stray marks. Then put your pencils down.**

After the test has been scored, review the questions and answer choices with students. If students are having difficulty, provide them with additional practice.

UNIT 10 Reference Materials

Lesson 23: Using a Table of Contents

Directions: Darken the circle for the correct answer.

TRY THIS	Study the table of contents shown on this page. Pay attention to chapter titles and page numbers. Be sure that you understand what kind of information can be found on the page.

S1

Canada: Land of Variety

CONTENTS

Chapter		Page
1	A Land of Immigrants	7
2	The Land and Its Resources	13
3	The People	27
4	Canada Before Confederation (Before 1867)	35
5	From Sea to Sea (1867 to the Present)	49
6	Canada's Government.................	59
7	How People Make a Living	69
8	Communities in Canada	81
9	Living in Canada.......................	111

Which chapter might tell about Canada during the 1700s?

A Chapter 1

B Chapter 2

C Chapter 4

D Chapter 6

THINK IT THROUGH	The correct answer is C. Since the title of Chapter 4 specifically states *(Before 1867)*, Chapter 4 would have information about Canada before 1867.

STOP

Use the table of contents in S1 to answer questions 1–4.

1 Which chapter might have information about the kinds of minerals found in Canada?

A Chapter 2   C Chapter 6

B Chapter 3   D Chapter 7

2 What information would be found in Chapter 6?

J The climate in Canada

K Canada in the 1920s

L The laws of Canada

M Popular sports in Canada

3 Which chapter might tell most about how Canadians celebrate certain holidays?

A Chapter 1   C Chapter 8

B Chapter 5   D Chapter 9

4 On what page would you begin reading to find out about immigrants to Canada?

J Page 7

K Page 35

L Page 59

M Page 81

STOP

Answers
S1 Ⓐ Ⓑ ● Ⓓ   2 Ⓙ Ⓚ ● Ⓜ   4 ● Ⓚ Ⓛ Ⓜ
1 ● Ⓑ Ⓒ Ⓓ   3 Ⓐ Ⓑ Ⓒ ●

Level 11

55

UNIT 10 Reference Materials

Lesson 23: Using a Table of Contents

Study Skill: Using a table of contents to find and determine information

SAY: **Turn to Lesson 23, Using a Table of Contents, on page 55.**

Check to see that all students find Lesson 23.

SAY: **In Lesson 23 you will practice using a table of contents to find information.**

Read the <u>Directions</u> to students.

SAY: **Now look at <u>Try This</u>.**

Read <u>Try This</u> to students.

SAY: **Now look at S1. Study the table of contents. Then read the question and answer choices carefully. Then darken the circle for the chapter that might tell about Canada during the 1700s.**

Allow students time to find and mark their answer.

SAY: **Now look at <u>Think It Through</u>.**

Read <u>Think It Through</u> to students. Check to see that students have filled in the correct answer space. Ask students if they have any questions.

SAY: **Now you will practice using a table of contents to find more information. Do numbers 1 through 4 just as we did S1. When you come to the word *STOP* at the bottom of page 55, put your pencils down. You may now begin.**

Allow students time to find and mark their answers.

Review the questions and answer choices with students. Discuss with the class why one answer is correct and the others are not correct. Also check to see that students have carefully filled in the answer space and have completely erased any stray marks.

66   Level 11

Directions: Choose the word or name that would come first if the words in each group were put in alphabetical order. Darken the circle for the correct answer.

> **TRY THIS**
> Carefully study each group of four words or names. Remember that two or more words in a list may have the same first letters. Then compare the next letters that are different.

S1
- A betray
- B bitter
- C butterfly
- D bonnet

> **THINK IT THROUGH**
> The correct answer is A. Because all the words begin with the letter *b*, you must look at the next letter in each word. The letter *e* comes before the letters *i*, *o*, and *u*.

STOP

1
- A gaudy
- B gaunt
- C gaucho
- D gauge

2
- J promenade
- K prominent
- L pronounce
- M promotion

3
- A scuffle
- B scroll
- C script
- D scrub

4
- J frown
- K fruit
- L fudge
- M frost

5
- A cancel
- B canary
- C candle
- D cannon

6
- J reply
- K replenish
- L replica
- M replace

7
- A visitor
- B vise
- C visor
- D vision

8
- J Afghanistan
- K Alaska
- L Aruba
- M Argentina

9
- A Jones, William
- B Jones, Wesley
- C Jones, Ward
- D Jones, Walter

10
- J blunder
- K bluff
- L blush
- M blur

11
- A lost
- B loop
- C loose
- D loom

12
- J Illinois Crime Commission
- K Illinois Commerce Commission
- L Illinois Youth Commission
- M Illinois Human Rights Commission

STOP

Answers

S1 ● Ⓑ Ⓒ Ⓓ 3 Ⓐ Ⓑ ● Ⓓ 6 Ⓙ Ⓚ Ⓛ ● 9 Ⓐ Ⓑ Ⓒ ● 12 Ⓙ ● Ⓛ Ⓜ
1 Ⓐ Ⓑ ● Ⓓ 4 Ⓙ Ⓚ Ⓛ ● 7 Ⓐ ● Ⓒ Ⓓ 10 Ⓙ ● Ⓛ Ⓜ
2 ● Ⓚ Ⓛ Ⓜ 5 Ⓐ ● Ⓒ Ⓓ 8 ● Ⓚ Ⓛ Ⓜ 11 Ⓐ Ⓑ Ⓒ ●

Level 11

56

Lesson 24: Alphabetizing

Study Skill: Alphabetizing beyond the first letter of a given word

SAY: **Turn to Lesson 24, Alphabetizing, on page 56.**

Check to see that all students find Lesson 24.

SAY: **In Lesson 24 you will practice alphabetizing beyond the first letter of a given word.**

Read the <u>Directions</u> to students.

SAY: **Now look at <u>Try This</u>.**

Read <u>Try This</u> to students.

SAY: **Now look at S1. Look at the group of four words. Darken the circle for the word that would come <u>first</u> if the words were arranged in alphabetical order.**

Allow students time to find and mark their answer.

SAY: **Now look at <u>Think It Through</u>.**

Read <u>Think It Through</u> to students. Check to see that students have filled in the correct answer space. Ask students if they have any questions.

SAY: **Now you will practice alphabetizing more groups of words or names beyond the first letter. Do numbers 1 through 12 just as we did S1. When you come to the word *STOP* at the bottom of page 56, put your pencils down. You may now begin.**

Allow students time to find and mark their answers.

Review the questions and answer choices with students. Discuss with the class why one answer is correct and the others are not correct. Also check to see that students have carefully filled in the answer space and have completely erased any stray marks.

Lesson 25: Using Reference Materials

Directions: Darken the circle for the correct answer.

| TRY THIS | First, think about the type of information you need. Then consider the encyclopedia volume that is the best source for the information. |

S1

Which volume would have the most information on reels, leaders, bait, and other fishing equipment?

A Volume 2

B Volume 4

C Volume 6

D Volume 10

| THINK IT THROUGH | The correct answer is B, Volume 4. To find out about fishing equipment, look up *fishing* in Volume 4, which has the letters *E–F*. |

STOP

Use the set of encyclopedias in S1 to answer questions 1–6.

1 Which volume might explain the ideas of Polish astronomer Nicolaus Copernicus?

A Volume 1   C Volume 8

B Volume 3   D Volume 9

2 Which volume might compare polar, grizzly, and Kodiak bears?

J Volume 2   L Volume 6

K Volume 5   M Volume 9

3 Which volume might compare methods of disposing of nuclear waste in Russia and the United States?

A Volume 4   C Volume 10

B Volume 8   D Volume 11

4 Which volume might have information about Mount Everest, on the border between China and Nepal?

J Volume 3   L Volume 7

K Volume 5   M Volume 8

5 Which volume might have information about French painter Claude Monet?

A Volume 3   C Volume 7

B Volume 4   D Volume 9

6 Which volume might have information about the climate in the Hawaiian Islands?

J Volume 3   L Volume 11

K Volume 5   M Volume 12

STOP

Level 11

57

Answers

S1 Ⓐ ● Ⓒ Ⓓ   2 ● Ⓚ Ⓛ Ⓜ   4 Ⓙ Ⓚ ● Ⓜ   6 Ⓙ ● Ⓛ Ⓜ

1 Ⓐ ● Ⓒ Ⓓ   3 Ⓐ ● Ⓒ Ⓓ   5 Ⓐ Ⓑ ● Ⓓ

Lesson 25: Using Reference Materials

Study Skill: Identifying the appropriate encyclopedia volume to use to locate specific information

SAY: **Turn to Lesson 25, Using Reference Materials, on page 57.**

Check to see that all students find Lesson 25.

SAY: **In Lesson 25 you will practice identifying the appropriate encyclopedia volume to use to locate specific information.**

Read the Directions to students.

SAY: **Now look at Try This.**

Read Try This to students.

SAY: **Now look at S1. Read the question and answer choices carefully. Then darken the circle for the volume that would have the most information on reels, leaders, bait, and other fishing equipment.**

Allow students time to find and mark their answer.

SAY: **Now look at Think It Through.**

Read Think It Through to students. Check to see that students have filled in the correct answer space. Ask students if they have any questions.

SAY: **Now you will practice identifying the appropriate encyclopedia volume to use to locate other specific information. Do number 1 through 6 just as we did S1. When you come to the word *STOP* at the bottom of page 57, put your pencils down. You may now begin.**

Allow students time to find and mark their answers.

Review the questions and answer choices with students. Discuss with the class why one answer is correct and the others are not correct. Also check to see that students have carefully filled in the answer space and have completely erased any stray marks.

Lesson 26: Using the Dictionary

Directions: Study the sample dictionary, the guide words, and the pronunciation key shown on this page. Read the questions and the answer choices carefully. Then darken the circle for the correct answer.

> **TRY THIS**
> Remember that entry words in a dictionary are listed in alphabetical order. Read all the definitions of the entry word. Study the pronunciation guide and the meaning of the abbreviations.

S1 What is the plural of the word *ambiguity*?

A ambiguitys

B ambiguityes

C ambiguities

D ambiguites

THINK IT THROUGH The correct answer is C. The plural of the word am**bi**guity is listed after the abbreviation *pl.*, which refers to the *plural* of the word.

STOP

---

adorn • aromatic

a•dorn (ə dôrn´) *v.* To decorate with something beautiful: *adorn fingers with rings.*

ad•sorb (ad sôrb´, ad zôrb´) *v.* To attract and hold (a substance) on a surface instead of absorbing it: *Platinum adsorbs hydrogen.*

ad•vance (ad vans´) *v.* To move forward, onward, or ahead. —*n.* Money given ahead of time. *Can you get an advance on your pay?*

air•wor•thy (âr´ wûr thē) *adj.* Ready for and capable of flight: *an airworthy airplane.*

al•a•bas•ter (al´ ə bas tər) *n.* Any of various hard, often tinted or banded minerals that consist mainly of salts of calcium.

a•lac•ri•ty (ə lak´ ri tē) *n.* speed and willingness in acting or responding: *He carried out the assignment with alacrity.*

am•bi•gu•i•ty (am bi gu´ i tē) *n., pl.* **am•bi•gu•i•ties. 1.** The condition of being ambiguous. **2.** Something that has two or more possible meanings. *There were numerous ambiguities in his statement.*

am•bush (am´ bush) *n.* **1.** A surprise attack made from a hiding place. **2.** A hidden place from which a surprise attack is made or planned.

ar•o•mat•ic (ar ə mat´ ik) *adj.* Having an aroma; fragrant.

---

1. Pronunciation Key

a	at	o	hot	u	pull
ā	ape	ō	old	û	turn
ä	far	ô	song	ch	chin
â	care	ô	fork	ng	sing
e	end	oi	oil	sh	shop
ē	me	ou	out	th	thin
i	it	u	up	th	this
ī	ice	ū	use	hw	in white
î	pierce	ü	rule	zh	in treasure

The ə symbol stands for the unstressed vowel heard in about, taken, pencil, lemon, and circus.

2. Abbreviations: *n.*, noun; *v.*, verb; *adj.*, adjective; *pl.*, plural.

GO ON

Level 11

Answer
S1 Ⓐ Ⓑ ● Ⓓ

58

Lesson 26: Using the Dictionary

Study Skill: Obtaining information by interpreting dictionary entries

SAY: **Turn to Lesson 26, Using the Dictionary, on page 58.**

Check to see that all students find Lesson 26.

SAY: **In Lesson 26 you will practice getting information from a dictionary by interpreting dictionary entries.**

Read the <u>Directions</u> to students.

SAY: **Now look at <u>Try This</u>.**

Read <u>Try This</u> to students.

SAY: **Look at S1. Study the sample dictionary and the pronunciation key shown on this page.** (Allow students a minute or two to study the sample dictionary and the pronunciation key.) **Read the question and answer choices carefully. Then darken the circle for the plural of the word *ambiguity*.**

Allow students time to find and mark their answer.

SAY: **Now look at <u>Think It Through</u>.**

Read <u>Think It Through</u> to students. Check to see that students have filled in the correct answer space. Ask students if they have any questions.

SAY: **Now you will practice obtaining more information from a dictionary. Do numbers 1 through 10 just as we did S1. When you come to the words *GO ON* at the bottom of page 58, continue working on the next page. When you come to the word *STOP* at the bottom of page 59, put your pencils down. You may now begin.**

Allow students time to find and mark their answers.

Use the sample dictionary and pronunciation key on page 58 to answer questions 1–10.

1 How should the word that means "fragrant" be spelled?

A aroematic   C arommatic

B aromatic   D aromattic

2 Which syllable of *alabaster* is accented?

J The first   L The third

K The second   M The fourth

3 The *a* in *adorn* sounds like the *o* in

A adsorb.   C airworthy.

B adorn.   D aromatic.

4 Which sentence correctly uses a form of the word *alacrity*?

J There was a large amount of *alacrity* in what he wrote.

K Jeannette finished her homework with *alacrity*.

L The sculptor added *alacrity* to the clay mixture.

M Raymond *alacritied* to the next level of baseball.

5 The *y* in *airworthy* sounds like the

A *a* in adorn.   C *e* in alabaster.

B *u* in ambush.   D *y* in ambiguity.

6 Which word describes an airplane that is ready for takeoff?

J alabaster   L airworthy

K alacrity   M ambush

7 Which word best fits in the sentence "Kelly liked to _____ herself with jewelry"?

A ambush

B adsorb

C adorn

D advance

8 A surprise attack by an army is an example of an

J ambush.   L adorn.

K adsorb.   M advance.

9 Which syllable of *alacrity* is accented?

A The first

B The second

C The third

D The fourth

10 How should the word that means "to attract and hold on a surface" be spelled?

J adssorb   L adsorbe

K addsorb   M adsorb

STOP

Answers

1 Ⓐ ● Ⓒ Ⓓ   3 Ⓐ Ⓑ Ⓒ ●   5 Ⓐ Ⓑ Ⓒ ●   7 Ⓐ Ⓑ ● Ⓓ   9 Ⓐ ● Ⓒ Ⓓ

2 ● Ⓚ Ⓛ Ⓜ   4 Ⓙ ● Ⓛ Ⓜ   6 Ⓙ Ⓚ ● Ⓜ   8 ● Ⓚ Ⓛ Ⓜ   10 Ⓙ Ⓚ Ⓛ ●

Lesson 27: Using the Library

Directions: Darken the circle for the correct answer.

TRY THIS	Think about the type of information you are seeking. This will help you decide which reference source to use.

S1 Which would most likely have information about population growth in India for the past five years?

A An atlas

B A globe

C An encyclopedia

D An almanac

THINK IT THROUGH	The correct answer is D. An almanac gives an overview of facts, often in chart or graph form. A globe is a model of the earth, an atlas shows maps of places on the earth, and an encyclopedia gives summaries of information.

STOP

1 Which source would you use when writing a report about the Civil War?

A An encyclopedia

B A dictionary

C A newspaper

D A history magazine

2 Which would show how to correctly divide the word *enterprise* at the end of a line?

J A thesaurus

K A dictionary

L An almanac

M An atlas

3 Which of the following would most likely be discussed in a history book?

A The difference between arteries and veins

B The correct way to write a letter

C The causes of World War I

D The different kinds of rocks

4 Which of the following would you find in the glossary of a book about nutrition?

J The page number on which the basic food groups are discussed

K The titles of the book's chapters

L A definition of the term *vitamin*

M A list of books about various foods

5 In which section of a library would you find a biography of John F. Kennedy?

A Nonfiction

B Fiction

C Reference

D Periodicals

6 Which magazine would most likely have a story about the Great Barrier Reef off the coast of Australia?

J *Reader's Digest*

K *Stereo Review*

L *Sports Illustrated*

M *National Geographic*

GO ON

Level 11

Answers

S1 Ⓐ Ⓑ Ⓒ ● 　 2 Ⓙ ● Ⓛ Ⓜ 　 4 Ⓙ Ⓚ ● Ⓜ 　 6 Ⓙ Ⓚ Ⓛ ●

1 ● Ⓑ Ⓒ Ⓓ 　 3 Ⓐ Ⓑ ● Ⓓ 　 5 ● Ⓑ Ⓒ Ⓓ

60

Lesson 27: Using the Library

Study Skills: Choosing appropriate reference materials to gather specific information; using a card catalog

SAY: **Turn to Lesson 27, Using the Library, on page 60.**

Check to see that all students find Lesson 27.

SAY: **In Lesson 27 you will practice choosing the appropriate reference material to use to find certain information, and practice interpreting information on a library catalog card.**

Read the Directions to students.

SAY: **Now look at Try This.**

Read Try This to students.

SAY: **Now look at S1. Read the question and answer choice. Then darken the circle for the reference source that would most likely have information about population growth in India for the past five years.**

Allow students time to find and mark their answer.

SAY: **Now look at Think It Through.**

Read Think It Through to students. Check to see that students have filled in the correct answer space. Ask students if they have any questions.

SAY: **Now you will practice choosing more appropriate reference materials to use to find information and you will practice interpreting more information on library catalog cards. Do numbers 1 through 16 just as we did S1. When you come to the words *GO ON* at the bottom of page 60, continue working on the next page. When you come to the word *STOP* at the bottom of page 61, put your pencils down. You may now begin.**

Allow students time to find and mark their answers.

Use the library catalog card shown here to answer questions 9–16.

VIETNAM

612.48 Luong, Quy
L   Remembering Vietnam / by Quy
        Luong; illustrated by Thuy Dang.
        – San Francisco: Freedom Rings
        Press, 1990.
        47 p.: ill.; 23 cm.

        1. Vietnam. I. Luong, Quy. II. Title.

---

9 **Who is the author of the book?**

A Thuy Dang

B Freedom Rings Press

C Quy Luong

D San Francisco

10 **Why is San Francisco listed on the card?**

J The book was published there.

K The author lives there.

L The illustrator took pictures there.

M Many Vietnamese people live there.

11 **The title of the book is**

A Freedom Rings Press.

B Vietnam.

C Remembering Vietnam.

D Quy Luong.

12 **What key word does the card tell you to use to find other books about Vietnam?**

J Geography

K Asia

L Title

M Vietnam

13 **Thuy Dang is the person who**

A edited the book.

B published the book.

C provided the pictures in the book.

D wrote the book.

14 **What does 1990 represent?**

J The year the author started the book

K The year the illustrator drew the pictures

L The year the book was written

M The year the book was published

15 **Who published this book?**

A Quy Luong

B Freedom Rings Press

C Thuy Dang

D San Francisco

16 **Which number tells where to find this book in the library?**

J 612.48

K 1990

L 23

M 47

STOP

Answers

9 Ⓐ Ⓑ ● Ⓓ   11 Ⓐ Ⓑ ● Ⓓ   13 Ⓐ Ⓑ ● Ⓓ   15 Ⓐ ● Ⓒ Ⓓ

10 ● Ⓚ Ⓛ Ⓜ   12 Ⓙ Ⓚ Ⓛ ●   14 Ⓙ Ⓚ Ⓛ ●   16 ● Ⓚ Ⓛ Ⓜ

61

Unit 10 Test

A Study of the Moon

CONTENTS

S1 Which chapter would probably tell about the size of the craters on the moon's surface?

A Chapter 1   C Chapter 3
B Chapter 2   D Chapter 4

STOP

Use the following table of contents to answer questions 1–5.

Life at a Zoo

Contents

1 On what page would you begin reading to learn how zoos in North America obtain animals from zoos in Asia?

A Page 3
B Page 15
C Page 30
D Page 45

2 Which chapter might list zoos to visit in Europe?

J Chapter 1
K Chapter 2
L Chapter 3
M Chapter 5

3 Which chapter might explain a zookeeper's job?

A Chapter 1
B Chapter 2
C Chapter 3
D Chapter 4

4 What information might be found in Chapter 3?

J A description of zoos in early Greece and Rome
K A map of the San Diego Zoo, the largest zoo in the world
L An explanation of how zoos help preserve some animal species
M Information about the feeding of zoo animals

5 On what page should you begin reading to learn about early zoos in Egypt, China, and Greece?

A Page 3
B Page 15
C Page 30
D Page 45

GO ON

Level 11

Answers
S1 Ⓐ Ⓑ ● Ⓓ   2 Ⓙ Ⓚ ● Ⓜ   4 Ⓙ ● Ⓛ Ⓜ
1 Ⓐ Ⓑ Ⓒ ●   3 Ⓐ Ⓑ Ⓒ ●   5 ● Ⓑ Ⓒ Ⓓ

Unit 10 Test

SAY: **Turn to the Unit 10 Test on page 62.**

Check to see that all students find the Unit 10 Test.

SAY: **In this test you will use the study skills that we have practiced in this unit. Look at S1. Study the table of contents.** (Allow students a minute or two to study the table of contents.) **Now read the question. You are asked to identify the chapter that would probably tell about the size of the craters on the moon's surface. Darken the circle for the correct answer.**

Allow students time to find and mark their answer.

SAY: **You should have darkened the circle for *C, Chapter 3*. Chapter 3 is entitled "The Surface of the Moon." This chapter is more likely to have information on the size of the craters on the moon than any other chapter listed in the table of contents.**

Check to see that all students have filled in the correct answer space. Ask students if they have any questions.

SAY: **Now you will finish the test on your own. Do numbers 1 through 20 just as we did S1. Read the questions and answer choices carefully. Study the visual materials. Then darken the circle for each correct answer. When you come to the words *GO ON* at the bottom of a page, continue working on the next page. When you come to the word *STOP* at the bottom of page 64, put your pencils down. You may now begin.**

Allow students time to find and mark their answers.

A Study of the Moon

CONTENTS

S1 Which chapter would probably tell about the size of the craters on the moon's surface?

A Chapter 1   C Chapter 3
B Chapter 2   D Chapter 4

STOP

Use the following table of contents to answer questions 1–5.

Life at a Zoo

Contents

1 On what page would you begin reading to learn how zoos in North America obtain animals from zoos in Asia?

A Page 3
B Page 15
C Page 30
D Page 45

2 Which chapter might list zoos to visit in Europe?

J Chapter 1
K Chapter 2
L Chapter 3
M Chapter 5

3 Which chapter might explain a zookeeper's job?

A Chapter 1
B Chapter 2
C Chapter 3
D Chapter 4

4 What information might be found in Chapter 3?

J A description of zoos in early Greece and Rome
K A map of the San Diego Zoo, the largest zoo in the world
L An explanation of how zoos help preserve some animal species
M Information about the feeding of zoo animals

5 On what page should you begin reading to learn about early zoos in Egypt, China, and Greece?

A Page 3
B Page 15
C Page 30
D Page 45

GO ON

Answers

For questions 6–10, choose the word or name that would appear **first** if the four words or names were arranged in alphabetical order.

6   J   attack
    K   attend
    L   attempt
    M   attach

7   A   Richards, Marjorie
    B   Ritchard, Mary
    C   Richardson, Michael
    D   Richards, Mark

8   J   emphasis
    K   embroider
    L   embassy
    M   embarrass

9   A   Dodge Feed Store
    B   Dodge Hardware
    C   Dodge Lumber Factory
    D   Dodge Paper Products

10 J   parasol
    K   paramedic
    L   parish
    M   paramount

Use the set of encyclopedias shown here to answer questions 11–14.

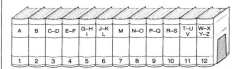

11 Which volume might have information about the history of the Red Cross in the United States?

    A   Volume 4
    B   Volume 8
    C   Volume 10
    D   Volume 11

12 Which volume might explain the inventions of Renaissance artist and scientist Leonardo da Vinci?

    J   Volume 1
    K   Volume 3
    L   Volume 5
    M   Volume 10

13 Which volume might describe the voyages of Christopher Columbus?

    A   Volume 3
    B   Volume 8
    C   Volume 9
    D   Volume 11

14 Which volume might have information about African-American baseball player Jackie Robinson?

    J   Volume 1
    K   Volume 2
    L   Volume 6
    M   Volume 10

GO ON

Level 11

Answers
6 ⓙ ⓚ ⓛ ●   8 ⓙ ⓚ ⓛ ●   10 ⓙ ● ⓛ ⓜ   12 ⓙ ● ⓛ ⓜ   14 ⓙ ⓚ ⓛ ●
7 ● Ⓑ Ⓒ Ⓓ   9 ● Ⓑ Ⓒ Ⓓ   11 Ⓐ Ⓑ ● Ⓓ   13 ● Ⓑ Ⓒ Ⓓ

63

Use the sample dictionary and the pronunciation key shown here to answer questions 15 and 16.

fettle • frailty

fet•tle (fet´ əl) *n.* Proper or sound condition; good spirits.

fi•as•co (fē as´ kō) *n. pl.* fi•as•coes or fi•as•cos. A complete failure: *His new book was the worst fiasco of the writer's career.*

fib (fib) *n.* A small or trivial lie.

foy•er (foi´ ər) *n.* 1. The lobby of a public building. 2. The entrance hall of a private house or apartment.

frail•ty (frāl´ tē) *n. pl.* frailties. The condition of being frail; weakness, especially of morality or character.

1. Pronunciation Key

a	at	o	hot	u̇	pull
ā	ape	ō	old	û	turn
ä	far	ô	song	ch	chin
â	care	ô	fork	ng	sing
e	end	oi	oil	sh	shop
ē	me	ou	out	th	thin
i	it	u	up	th	this
ī	ice	ū	use	hw	in white
î	pierce	ü	rule	zh	in treasure

The ə symbol stands for the unstressed vowel heard in about, taken, pencil, lemon, and circus.

2. Abbreviations: *n.*, noun; *v.*, verb; *adj.*, adjective; *pl.*, plural.

15 The *y* in *frailty* sounds like the

   A *i* in fib.   C *e* in fettle.

   B *i* in fiasco.   D *e* in foyer.

16 How should the word that means "good spirits" be spelled?

   J fetle   L fettel

   K fetel   M fettle

For questions 17 and 18, darken the circle for the correct answer.

17 Which of these would tell you about the history of Spain?

   A A dictionary

   B An encyclopedia

   C A newspaper

   D An atlas

18 Which of these would you find in the table of contents of a book about explorers?

   J The titles of the book's chapters

   K A list of explorers

   L A list of books about famous explorers

   M A definition of the word *conquistador*

Use the library catalog card shown here to answer questions 19 and 20.

AMERICAN FLAG
712.0   Rider, Emily J.
R   History of the American Flag / by Emily J. Rider; photographs by Bob Patterson. – Bishop City, Iowa: American Press, 1990. 323 p.: ill.
1. American History. 2. Flags. 3. American Flag. I. Title.

19 Emily Rider is the

   A publisher of the book.

   B photographer of the book.

   C editor of the book.

   D author of the book.

20 What is the title of the book?

   J American Flag

   K History of the American Flag

   L American Press

   M Flags

STOP

Level 11

Answers

15 Ⓐ ● Ⓒ Ⓓ   17 Ⓐ ● Ⓒ Ⓓ   19 Ⓐ Ⓑ Ⓒ ●

64   16 Ⓙ Ⓚ Ⓛ ●   18 ● Ⓚ Ⓛ Ⓜ   20 Ⓙ ● Ⓛ Ⓜ

After the test has been scored, review the questions and answer choices with students. If students are having difficulty, provide them with additional practice.

Getting Ready for the Comprehensive Tests

The Comprehensive Tests are designed to simulate the Iowa Tests of Basic Skills. Each Comprehensive Test has a suggested time limit. It is recommended that you follow these time limits and that you schedule no more than three tests in one day, providing sufficient breaks between tests.

Following the suggestions presented here will enable students to experience test taking under the same structured conditions that apply when achievement tests are administered. Furthermore, students will have a final opportunity to apply the skills they have learned in *Test Best*, prior to taking the Iowa Tests Of Basic Skills.

The following table lists recommended test sessions and time limits for each test. The time noted is the approximate time needed to administer each of the Comprehensive Tests. It is suggested that you allow fifteen or twenty minutes for students to complete the personal information required on the *Test Best* Answer Sheet shown on pages 78 and 79 of this book and on the back cover of the student book.

Test Session	Comprehensive Test	Test Time
First Day	1—Vocabulary	15
	2—Reading Comprehension	20
	3—Spelling	15
Second Day	4—Language Mechanics	15
	5—Language Expression	20
Third Day	6—Math Concepts and Estimation	25
	7—Math Problems	15
	8—Math Computation	10
Fourth Day	9—Maps and Diagrams	20
	10—Reference Materials	20

Test Day

To simulate the structured atmosphere of the Iowa Tests of Basic Skills, take the following steps on the day of the test:

- Hang a "Do Not Disturb—Testing" sign on the classroom door to avoid interruptions.

- Use a stopwatch to accurately observe the time limit marked on each test.

- Remove the Answer Sheet (found on pages 93 and 94) from each *Test Best on the Iowa Tests of Basic Skills* book.

- Seat students at an appropriate distance from one another, and make sure that their desks are clear of all materials.

- Provide students with sharpened pencils that have erasers.

- Keep supplies, such as extra pencils and scratch paper for Tests 6, 7, and 8, readily available.

- Distribute the *Test Best* books to students, and encourage them to do their best.

Before you begin, remind students to press firmly with their pencils to make a dark mark. Remind students of the importance of completely filling in the answer spaces and erasing any stray marks that might be picked up as answers by the scoring machines.

While you are administering the Comprehensive Tests, make sure that students understand the directions before proceeding with each test. Circulate around the classroom, making sure that students are following the directions, that they are working on the appropriate test, and that they are marking their Answer Sheets properly. Check to see that students have carefully filled in the answer spaces and have completely erased any stray marks.

Answer Sheet

STUDENT'S NAME

LAST		FIRST		MI	SCHOOL:
					TEACHER:

FEMALE ○   MALE ○

(Name grid: columns of bubbles A–Z with empty circle at top of each column)

BIRTH DATE

MONTH	DAY		YEAR	
Jan ○	⓪	⓪	⓪	⓪
Feb ○	①	①	①	①
Mar ○	②	②	②	②
Apr ○	③	③	③	③
May ○		④	④	④
Jun ○		⑤	⑤	⑤
Jul ○		⑥	⑥	⑥
Aug ○		⑦	⑦	⑦
Sep ○		⑧	⑧	⑧
Oct ○		⑨	⑨	⑨
Nov ○				
Dec ○				

GRADE ③ ④ ⑤ ⑥ ⑦ ⑧

TEST BEST
ON THE
IOWA TESTS OF BASIC SKILLS®

STECK-VAUGHN
COMPANY

Iowa Tests of Basic Skills® is a trademark of the Riverside Publishing Company. Such company has neither endorsed nor authorized this test-preparation book.

TEST 1   Vocabulary

S1 ● Ⓑ Ⓒ Ⓓ	5 Ⓐ Ⓑ Ⓒ ●	10 Ⓙ Ⓚ ● Ⓜ	15 Ⓐ ● Ⓒ Ⓓ	20 ● Ⓚ Ⓛ Ⓜ	25 Ⓐ Ⓑ Ⓒ ●
1 Ⓐ Ⓑ ● Ⓓ	6 Ⓙ Ⓚ ● Ⓜ	11 Ⓐ Ⓑ ● Ⓓ	16 Ⓙ Ⓚ ● Ⓜ	21 Ⓐ ● Ⓒ Ⓓ	26 Ⓙ Ⓚ ● Ⓜ
2 Ⓙ Ⓚ ● Ⓜ	7 ● Ⓑ Ⓒ Ⓓ	12 Ⓙ Ⓚ Ⓛ ●	17 ● Ⓑ Ⓒ Ⓓ	22 ● Ⓚ Ⓛ Ⓜ	27 ● Ⓑ Ⓒ Ⓓ
3 ● Ⓑ Ⓒ Ⓓ	8 ● Ⓚ Ⓛ Ⓜ	13 Ⓐ ● Ⓒ Ⓓ	18 Ⓙ Ⓚ Ⓛ ●	23 Ⓐ ● Ⓒ Ⓓ	28 Ⓙ Ⓚ ● Ⓜ
4 ● Ⓚ Ⓛ Ⓜ	9 Ⓐ ● Ⓒ Ⓓ	14 ● Ⓚ Ⓛ Ⓜ	19 Ⓐ Ⓑ ● Ⓓ	24 Ⓙ ● Ⓛ Ⓜ	

TEST 2   Reading Comprehension

S1 Ⓐ ● Ⓒ Ⓓ	4 Ⓙ Ⓚ ● Ⓜ	8 ● Ⓚ Ⓛ Ⓜ	12 Ⓙ ● Ⓛ Ⓜ	16 Ⓙ ● Ⓛ Ⓜ	20 Ⓙ Ⓚ ● Ⓜ
1 Ⓐ Ⓑ Ⓒ ●	5 Ⓐ Ⓑ ● Ⓓ	9 ● Ⓑ Ⓒ Ⓓ	13 ● Ⓑ Ⓒ Ⓓ	17 Ⓐ Ⓑ Ⓒ ●	
2 ● Ⓚ Ⓛ Ⓜ	6 Ⓙ Ⓚ Ⓛ ●	10 Ⓙ Ⓚ ● Ⓜ	14 Ⓙ Ⓚ Ⓛ ●	18 Ⓙ Ⓚ Ⓛ ●	
3 Ⓐ Ⓑ Ⓒ ●	7 Ⓐ ● Ⓒ Ⓓ	11 Ⓐ Ⓑ Ⓒ ●	15 ● Ⓑ Ⓒ Ⓓ	19 Ⓐ ● Ⓒ Ⓓ	

TEST 3   Spelling

S1 Ⓐ Ⓑ Ⓒ Ⓓ ●	6 Ⓙ Ⓚ Ⓛ ● Ⓝ	12 ● Ⓚ Ⓛ Ⓜ Ⓝ	18 ● Ⓚ Ⓛ Ⓜ Ⓝ	24 Ⓙ Ⓚ ● Ⓜ Ⓝ	30 Ⓙ ● Ⓛ Ⓜ Ⓝ
1 Ⓐ Ⓑ ● Ⓓ Ⓔ	7 Ⓐ ● Ⓒ Ⓓ Ⓔ	13 Ⓐ Ⓑ Ⓒ ● Ⓔ	19 Ⓐ Ⓑ Ⓒ ● Ⓔ	25 ● Ⓑ Ⓒ Ⓓ Ⓔ	31 Ⓐ Ⓑ Ⓒ ● Ⓔ
2 ● Ⓚ Ⓛ Ⓜ Ⓝ	8 Ⓙ Ⓚ ● Ⓜ Ⓝ	14 Ⓙ Ⓚ Ⓛ ● Ⓝ	20 Ⓙ ● Ⓛ Ⓜ Ⓝ	26 Ⓙ Ⓚ ● Ⓜ Ⓝ	32 Ⓙ Ⓚ Ⓛ Ⓜ ●
3 ● Ⓑ Ⓒ Ⓓ Ⓔ	9 Ⓐ Ⓑ Ⓒ ● Ⓔ	15 Ⓐ ● Ⓒ Ⓓ Ⓔ	21 Ⓐ Ⓑ Ⓒ ● Ⓔ	27 Ⓐ Ⓑ Ⓒ ● Ⓔ	33 Ⓐ Ⓑ Ⓒ ● Ⓔ
4 Ⓙ Ⓚ ● Ⓜ Ⓝ	10 Ⓙ Ⓚ Ⓛ Ⓜ ●	16 ● Ⓚ Ⓛ Ⓜ Ⓝ	22 Ⓙ Ⓚ ● Ⓜ Ⓝ	28 Ⓙ Ⓚ ● Ⓜ Ⓝ	34 Ⓙ ● Ⓛ Ⓜ Ⓝ
5 Ⓐ Ⓑ Ⓒ Ⓓ ●	11 Ⓐ ● Ⓒ Ⓓ Ⓔ	17 Ⓐ Ⓑ Ⓒ ● Ⓔ	23 ● Ⓑ Ⓒ Ⓓ Ⓔ	29 Ⓐ Ⓑ Ⓒ ● Ⓔ	

CUT HERE

Level 11   **93**

Preparing the *Test Best* Answer Sheet

Distribute a *Test Best* Answer Sheet to each student. Refer to the *Test Best* Answer Sheet shown on this page and have students complete the required personal data. Use the procedures below to properly mark the personal data on the Answer Sheet. This will help ensure that students' test results will be properly recorded.

SAY: **Before we begin with Test 1 of the Comprehensive Tests, we need to complete some information on the *Test Best* Answer Sheet. We will do this together now. Make sure that you are looking at page 93, with the heading *STUDENT'S NAME* at the top of the page. Just below this at the left is the heading *LAST*. In the boxes under *LAST*, print your last name—one letter in each box. Print as many letters as will fit. In the boxes under *FIRST*, print your first name—one letter in each box. Print as many letters as will fit. If you have a middle name, print your middle initial in the *MI* box. Leave the *MI* box empty if you do not have a middle name.**

Allow students time to print their names.

SAY: **Now look at the columns of letters below each of the boxes. In each column, darken the circle that matches the letter in that box. Darken the empty circle at the top of the column if there i no letter in the box.**

Allow students time to darken the circles. Circulate around the classroom to make sure that students are completing the appropriate part of the Answer Sheet.

SAY: **Now look at the top right side of your Answer Sheet where it lists *SCHOOL* and *TEACHER*.**

Print the school's name and your name on the chalkboard and allow students time to copy this information onto their Answer Sheets.

TEST 4 — Language Mechanics

S1 ●BCD	4 ●KLM	9 A●CD	14 JK●M	19 ABC●	24 JKL●
S2 ●KLM	5 A●CD	10 ●KLM	15 A●CD	20 J●LM	
1 A●CD	6 JK●M	11 AB●D	16 J●LM	21 ABC●	
2 JKL●	7 AB●D	12 JK●M	17 ●BCD	22 JK●M	
3 AB●D	8 J●LM	13 ●BCD	18 J●LM	23 A●CD	

TEST 5 — Language Expression

S1 A●CD	6 ●KLM	12 J●LM	18 J●LM	24 ●KLM	30 JK●M
1 A●CD	7 AB●D	13 A●CD	19 AB●D	25 ABC●	31 ●BCD
2 JK●M	8 ●KLM	14 ●KLM	20 ●KLM	26 JKL●	32 JKL●
3 ABC●	9 A●CD	15 ●BCD	21 A●CD	27 ●KLM	33 AB●D
4 J●LM	10 ●KLM	16 JKL●	22 ●KLM	28 J●LM	
5 AB●D	11 AB●D	17 ●BCD	23 ABC●	29 ●BCD	

TEST 6 — Math Concepts and Estimation

S1 AB●D	6 ●KLM	12 ●KLM	18 JK●M	24 J●LM	30 JK●M
1 ●BCD	7 A●CD	13 A●CD	19 A●CD	25 AB●D	31 AB●D
2 JKL●	8 JKL●	14 ●KLM	20 JKL●	26 JK●M	32 JK●M
3 ABC●	9 AB●D	15 AB●D	21 A●CD	27 ABC●	33 AB●D
4 J●LM	10 J●LM	16 JK●M	22 JKL●	28 J●LM	34 JK●M
5 AB●D	11 ABC●	17 ABC●	23 A●CD	29 AB●D	

TEST 7 — Math Problems

S1 A●CD	3 ABC●	6 JK●M	9 A●CD	12 JK●M
1 AB●D	4 JK●M	7 A●CD	10 JKL●	
2 ●KLM	5 A●CD	8 J●LM	11 AB●D	

TEST 8 — Math Computation

S1 ●BCD	1 A●CD	3 ●BCD	5 ●BCD	7 AB●D	9 ●BCD
S2 JKL●	2 J●LM	4 ●KLM	6 J●LM	8 JK●M	10 JKL●

TEST 9 — Maps and Diagrams

S1 AB●D	3 ABC●	6 JKL●	9 AB●D	12 JK●M	15 AB●D
1 AB●D	4 JKL●	7 ●BCD	10 JKL●	13 A●CD	
2 J●LM	5 AB●D	8 JKL●	11 ●BCD	14 ●KLM	

TEST 10 — Reference Materials

S1 AB●D	5 ABC●	10 J●LM	15 ABC●	20 JK●M
1 ABC●	6 JK●M	11 A●CD	16 J●LM	21 A●CD
2 JK●M	7 ABC●	12 JKL●	17 A●CD	22 JKL●
3 ●BCD	8 J●LM	13 ABC●	18 JKL●	23 ABC●
4 JK●M	9 A●CD	14 JKL●	19 ABC●	24 J●LM

ISBN 0-8114-2862-1
90000
9 780811 428620

CUT HERE

94 Level 11

SAY: **Now look at the section directly below *TEACHER*. Darken the circle for *FEMALE* if you are a girl. Darken the circle for *MALE* if you are a boy. Then look at the *BIRTH DATE* section. Under *MONTH*, darken the circle for the month you were born. Under *DAY*, darken the circles that have the one or two numerals of the day you were born. If your birthday has only one numeral, darken the circle for zero in the first column of numerals. Under *YEAR* darken the circles for the last two numbers of the year you were born. Finally, under *GRADE*, darken the circle that has the number for your grade.**

Allow students time to complete the information. Remind students to press firmly on their pencils to make a dark mark. Check to see that students have carefully filled in the circles and have completely erased any stray marks. Remind students of the importance of completely filling the answer space and erasing any stray marks that might be picked up as answers by the scoring machines.

Comprehensive Tests

Test 1: Vocabulary

S1   **Raw** vegetables
A   uncooked
B   crunchy
C   sliced
D   pickled
STOP

For questions 1–28, darken the circle for the word or words that mean the <u>same</u> or <u>almost the same</u> as the word in dark type.

1   A **ridiculous** suggestion
A   thoughtless
B   sharp
C   foolish
D   serious

2   To show great **astonishment**
J   fear
K   happiness
L   surprise
M   hope

3   To **nestle**
A   snuggle
B   irritate
C   organize
D   misjudge

4   Offered a **vague** explanation
J   uncertain
K   cautious
L   capable
M   clear

5   To **gain** respect
A   fill
B   lose
C   change
D   earn

6   Signed a peace **pact**
J   stake
K   paper
L   agreement
M   sketch

7   Regarded as an **outcast**
A   displaced person
B   aftereffect
C   nozzle
D   old person

8   Delivered an **accurate** report
J   correct
K   exaggerated
L   incorrect
M   reliable

9   The **outskirts** of town
A   exterior
B   border
C   center
D   ledge

10   **Snug** clothing
J   cotton
K   warm
L   tight
M   loose

11   To live in **miserable** poverty
A   delighted
B   concerned
C   unhappy
D   angry

12   To be a **pacifist**
J   easily alarmed person
K   hateful person
L   careful person
M   peaceable person

13   **Opposing** the idea
A   supporting
B   voting against
C   making up
D   covering up

GO ON

Level 11

65

Comprehensive Tests

Test 1: Vocabulary

Allow 15 minutes for this test.

SAY: **Turn to Test 1, Vocabulary, on page 65.**

Check to see that all students find Test 1.

SAY: **In this test you will use your reading skills to answer questions. Look at S1. Read the phrase and answer choices carefully. Then darken the circle for the correct answer.**

Allow students time to find and mark their answer.

SAY: **You should have darkened the circle for A. The word** uncooke **means the same or almost the same as the word in dark type,** Raw**.**

Check to see that all students have filled in the correct answer space. As students if they have any questions.

SAY: **Now you will finish the test on your own. Read the directions carefully. Then do numbers 1 through 28 just as we did S1. Darken the circle for each correct answer. When you come to the words** GO ON **at the bottom of page 65, continue working on the next page. When you come to the word** STOP **at the bottom of page 66, put your pencils down. You have 15 minutes to complete the test. You may now begin.**

Allow students 15 minutes to find and mark their answers.

14 A **parched** landscape
   J dry
   K sore
   L harmless
   M humid

15 To **persecute** your enemy
   A convince
   B torment
   C murder
   D forgive

16 **Refunded** the deposit
   J cashed
   K leased
   L returned
   M recorded

17 A **complex** problem
   A hard to understand
   B popular
   C short
   D easy to solve

18 Very **grateful**
   J unsure
   K quiet
   L careful
   M thankful

19 **Numb** toes
   A many
   B warm
   C unfeeling
   D broken

20 A **dreary** old house
   J depressing
   K exciting
   L flat
   M inviting

21 The usual **routine**
   A criminal
   B method
   C fuss
   D route

22 A **humorous** story
   J funny
   K annoying
   L rude
   M independent

23 A **boring** excuse
   A sad
   B tiresome
   C interesting
   D long

24 **Absent** today
   J amateur
   K missing
   L present
   M clumsy

25 A decisive **victory**
   A view
   B leader
   C defeat
   D triumph

26 A **vast** parcel of land
   J green
   K wild
   L enormous
   M expensive

27 An **energetic** workout
   A vigorous
   B lazy
   C friendly
   D healthy

28 An educational **pamphlet**
   J committee
   K presentation
   L booklet
   M leader

STOP

It is now time to stop. You have completed Test 1. Make sure that you have carefully filled in your answer spaces and have completely erased any stray marks. Then put your pencils down and close your books.

After the test has been scored, review the questions and answer choices with students. If students are having difficulty with any lesson, provide them with additional practice items.

S1 I wanted to buy a new skateboard, but I didn't have enough money. So I asked my parents what I needed to do to increase my allowance. They added some chores to my weekly list and doubled my allowance. Within seven weeks I was able to buy the skateboard I wanted.

How did the author get the money needed to buy a new skateboard?

A Borrowed from her parents

B Did more chores to increase her allowance

C Found a part-time job

D Asked her sister for the money

STOP

For questions 1–20, darken the circle for the correct answer.

A visitor to a city in Bolivia, such as La Paz, might find the following recommendations in a brochure in the hotel room:

If it is your first day here in our lovely city, you must take it easy and rest. We recommend that you not walk for even short distances. You must not climb stairs.

These recommendations are posted in hotel rooms to help warn visitors of the potential hazards of a high altitude. You see, La Paz is located at a high altitude in the Andes Mountains. People who are not used to living at such altitudes can contract *sorojche*, or altitude sickness. Nausea, headaches, and tired muscles are some of the symptoms of this illness. These symptoms are caused by lack of oxygen from the thin air at high altitudes.

People who rent cars in La Paz are given containers of water to take with them. Car radiators quickly boil over in high altitudes because water boils at a lower temperature in high altitudes than in low altitudes. Water often needs to be replaced in radiators of cars driven at high altitudes.

1 La Paz is located high in the Andes Mountains in

A Brazil.

B Colombia.

C Mexico.

D Bolivia.

2 Why are visitors to La Paz given recommendations about what to do their first day in the city?

J So visitors do not get sick

K Visitors to La Paz usually get lost their first day in the city.

L It is part of the tradition in South American cities to make recommendations to visitors about what to do on their first day in a new city.

M The government of La Paz limits the activities of visitors on their first day in the city.

3 How do people get *sorojche*?

A By driving too fast

B From resting the first day they arrive in a city

C Buy it in a local store

D From too much activity the first day in a place at a high altitude

4 Why are people who rent cars in La Paz given containers of water to carry with them?

J The air is hot and people can get ill if they do not drink a lot of water.

K They are asked to water wilting plants along their trip.

L Cars in La Paz often need to have their radiators filled with water.

M People who rent cars in La Paz are required to keep their cars clean at all times.

GO ON

Level 11

67

Test 2: Reading Comprehension

Allow 20 minutes for this test.

SAY: **Turn to Test 2, Reading Comprehension, on page 67.**

Check to see that all students find Test 2.

SAY: **In this test you will use your reading skills to answer question about selections that you read. Look at S1. Read the selection the question, and the answer choices carefully. Then darken the circle for the correct answer.**

Allow students time to find and mark their answer.

SAY: **You should have darkened the circle for** *B* **because the selection states that the author's parents added more chores and doubled the author's allowance.**

Check to see that all students have filled in the correct answer space. Ask students if they have any questions.

SAY: **Now you will finish the test on your own. Do questions 1 through 20 just as we did S1. Darken the circle for each correct answer. When you come to the words** *GO ON* **at the bottom of a page, continue working on the next page. When you come to the word** *STOP* **at the bottom of page 71, put your pencils down. You have 20 minutes to complete the test. You may now begin.**

Allow students 20 minutes to find and mark their answers.

Here is a journal selection written by a boy on vacation.

August 5—My family and I spent the day packing for our canoe trip to the Boundary Waters Canoe Area (BWCA) in Minnesota. We have been planning this trip for the past six months. I hope the trip is worth all the time that we spent in preparation. We will leave tomorrow morning before daylight.

August 6—We got started early. We stopped at a canoe outfitters station along the way. There we rented two canoes for our trip. My older brother and I will use one canoe and my parents will use the other. It took eight hours to drive to the ranger station at the outskirts of the BWCA. There we met two other families that are traveling with us. The ranger asked us to watch a short video about the BWCA. It explained the rules for camping in the canoe area. Campsites are not reserved here. We were given a map showing the campsites. We decided to stay overnight in a cabin near the BWCA and rest for the canoe trip in the morning.

August 7—We drove a few miles down a very bumpy dirt road to a place where we could unload our cars and set off in our canoes. We canoed for about two hours before we got to our portage. In order to get to Lake Bruel, where we wanted to camp, we needed to move all our gear overland. Wow, what a tiring experience! I carried a backpack on my back and the front end of the canoe over my head for about a quarter of a mile. I was glad to settle back into the canoe on the other side of the portage.

The scenery along Lake Bruel was breathtaking. There were pine trees taller than most buildings back home. Loons and ducks were floating in large groups and calling to one another. We passed dams built by beavers. The lake water was so clear that I could see the bottom of the lake and the fish, plants, and bugs that live there. I love the quiet here and the close contact with nature.

Midday we spied a sandy beach on an island in the lake and decided to stop there for lunch. We ate, sunbathed, and swam. The water was ice cold, but it felt good since the temperature was hot.

It was late afternoon before we began canoeing again. We read our maps to find the campsites along the lake. The first three campsites we passed were already being used so we traveled on. Finally, the fourth site appeared to be empty so we searched the shore for the best place to land. First, we set up our tents. Next, we got our campfire started and fixed a hearty meal of hamburger, potatoes, carrots, onion, and a teaspoon of butter cooked together in aluminum foil. We were all hungry. Not a crumb was left. After dinner we cleaned our food area and then hung our food pack from a high branch to keep bears and other animals from eating our food. We spent some time around the campfire talking enthusiastically about previous camping trips we had taken together.

GO ON

5   According to the journal selection, the author's canoe trip to the Boundary Waters Canoe Area (BWCA) in Minnesota

A   was a last minute idea.

B   was planned the week before.

C   took six months to plan.

D   was a surprise for the author.

6   What information did the campers learn from the video that they watched at the ranger station?

J   How to choose a canoe

K   How to fish in deep lakes

L   An explanation of endangered species that live in the canoe area

M   An explanation of the rules for camping in the canoe area

7   How did the journal author probably feel after the portage?

A   Angry

B   Exhausted

C   Fearful

D   Confused

8   According to the author of the journal, Lake Bruel was

J   filled with animal life.

K   polluted.

L   filled with noisy motorboats.

M   boring because there was nothing to do there.

9   You can conclude from the journal selection that the season during which the author and his family and friends went canoeing and camping was most likely

A   summer.

B   winter.

C   spring.

D   autumn.

10   How did the journal author and his companions obtain their campsite?

J   They reserved it six months ahead of time.

K   They asked the ranger to pick a site for them.

L   They read a map showing campsites and canoed to an empty site.

M   They rented a site at the canoe outfitters station on the way to the BWCA.

11   What was the second thing that the campers did when they arrived at their campsite?

A   They took a nap.

B   They went for a swim.

C   They set up their tents.

D   They made a campfire.

12   How did the campers keep their food from being eaten by animals?

J   They stored it in the canoe.

K   They hung it from a high branch.

L   They put garlic on the outside of the food pack.

M   They sprayed the food pack with animal repellent.

GO ON

"Mom, look over there. Isn't that Jane Addams?" asked Erich.

"Yes, yes you are correct. That is Jane Addams. I would know her anywhere. She helped me settle into the American way of life when I first moved here from Germany," replied Mrs. Schroeder.

"What do you mean, Mom?" asked Erich.

"When I first came to Chicago in 1890 I could not speak any English. I did not have a job. I am afraid that I did not know anyone either. I was only 19 years old and I was determined to become an American citizen and become a successful person in the United States, but it was difficult. I heard about Jane Addams's Hull House from another German immigrant. She told me that I could go to Hull House and learn English and become accustomed to life in the United States," answered Mrs. Schroeder.

"Did you go to Hull House, Mom?" asked Erich.

"I went as soon as I could get there. I signed up for an evening class to learn English. The social workers at Hull House were able to get me a job, too. It was not a great job—I stocked shelves at a small local grocery store, but it was a living. The social workers also helped me find a safe place to live. I shared a room in an apartment with two other women about my age. It worked out fine." said Mrs. Schroeder.

"Did you ever talk to Jane Addams?" queried Erich.

"Jane Addams made it a point to talk to all the people who came to Hull House. After I finished my English classes, she asked to meet with me. She told me how I could become an American citizen. I took more classes at Hull House. This time I learned about the government of the United States. It was in this class that I met your father. He and I became American citizens in the same naturalization ceremony," explained Mrs. Schroeder.

"Why did Jane Addams help establish Hull House? She knew how to speak English," wondered Erich.

"She was a humanitarian. She saw a need for a community center that would help immigrants, young and old alike, from becoming impoverished and help them become upstanding American citizens. She is my hero." stated Mrs. Schroeder.

GO ON

Level 11

70

13 **Which is the best title for this passage?**

    A "Jane Addams and Hull House"

    B "The Life of Erich Schroeder"

    C "The History of Chicago"

    D "Immigrant Life"

14 **Why did Mrs. Schroeder come to the United States?**

    J She wanted to search for gold.

    K She hoped to learn to speak English.

    L She wanted a find a job in a grocery store.

    M She wanted to become a citizen of the United States.

15 **How did Mrs. Schroeder find out about Hull House?**

    A A German immigrant told Mrs. Schroeder about Hull House.

    B Mrs. Schroeder heard about Hull House when she still lived in Germany.

    C She read a newspaper article about Hull House and Jane Addams.

    D Jane Addams invited her to come to Hull House.

16 **What does the phrase "it was a living" mean in the sixth paragraph?**

    J It was a life-long dream.

    K It was a way to make money.

    L It was a safe place to live and raise a family.

    M It was too crowded to breathe.

17 **What did Mrs. Schroeder need to do in order to become a citizen of the United States?**

    A She needed to find a safe place to live.

    B She needed to get married.

    C She was required to have a well-paying job.

    D She had to learn about the government of the United States.

18 **Which word best describes Jane Addams?**

    J Pitiless

    K Rash

    L Wealthy

    M Compassionate

19 **What is the eighth paragraph mainly about?**

    A How Jane Addams established Hull House

    B How Mrs. Schroeder became an American citizen

    C How immigrants lived in Chicago

    D How Mrs. Schroeder first settled in the United States

20 **What does the word "impoverished" mean in the last paragraph?**

    J Affluent

    K Impossible

    L Poverty-stricken

    M Sent back to the mother country

STOP

Level 11

71

SAY: **It is now time to stop. You have completed Test 2. Make sure that you have carefully filled in your answer spaces and have completely erased any stray marks. Then put your pencils down and close your books.**

After the test has been scored, review the questions and answer choices with students. If students are having difficulty with any lesson, provide them with additional practice items.

S1
A alley
B affect
C compare
D squash
E (No mistakes)

STOP

For questions 1–34, darken the circle for word that is not spelled correctly. Darken the circle for *No mistakes* if all the words are spelled correctly.

1
A auditorium
B medicine
C intervle
D confident
E (No mistakes)

2
J pinapple
K vaccination
L semester
M reputation
N (No mistakes)

3
A sprayned
B bugle
C consult
D bathed
E (No mistakes)

4
J cement
K whiskers
L tenis
M cactus
N (No mistakes)

5
A student
B pirate
C landlord
D machinery
E (No mistakes)

6
J patio
K rungs
L rugged
M subjekt
N (No mistakes)

7
A regiment
B scrach
C textiles
D pierced
E (No mistakes)

8
J sketch
K cottage
L submurge
M bureau
N (No mistakes)

9
A sought
B voted
C coiled
D exspress
E (No mistakes)

10
J acquaint
K blunder
L contrary
M federal
N (No mistakes)

11
A situation
B cristal
C pronunciation
D blond
E (No mistakes)

12
J fasinate
K energy
L previous
M liable
N (No mistakes)

13
A dinosaur
B pansies
C jewelry
D genaration
E (No mistakes)

14
J determine
K inspect
L attract
M feminin
N (No mistakes)

15
A prevent
B enkourage
C rehearse
D dues
E (No mistakes)

16
J gilty
K helicopters
L mantels
M instructions
N (No mistakes)

GO ON
Level 11

72

Test 3: Spelling

Allow 15 minutes for this test.

SAY: **Turn to Test 3, Spelling, on page 72.**

Check to see that all students find Test 3.

SAY: **In this test you will use your language skills to find the correct spellings of words. Look at S1. Read the answer choices carefully. Then darken the circle for the word that is <u>not</u> spelled correctly. Darken the circle for *No mistakes* if all the words are spelled correctly.**

Allow students time to find and mark their answer.

SAY: **You should have darkened the circle for *E* because all of the words are spelled correctly.**

Check to see that all students have filled in the correct answer space. Ask students if they have any questions.

SAY: **Now you will finish the test on your own. Read the directions carefully. Then do numbers 1 through 34 just as we did S1. Darken the circle for each correct answer. When you come to the words *GO ON* at the bottom of page 72, continue working on the next page. When you come to the word *STOP* at the bottom of page 73, put your pencils down. You have 15 minutes to complete the test. You may now begin.**

Allow students 15 minutes to find and mark their answers.

17	A	knuckle	23	A	debait	29	A	transparent
	B	lather		B	tomatoes		B	magnificent
	C	youngster		C	majority		C	delegate
	D	wresle		D	scan		D	instructer
	E	*(No mistakes)*		E	*(No mistakes)*		E	*(No mistakes)*

18	J	empror	24	J	account	30	J	jagged
	K	wondrous		K	occasion		K	ovious
	L	versus		L	purfume		L	memories
	M	typhoon		M	regular		M	luggage
	N	*(No mistakes)*		N	*(No mistakes)*		N	*(No mistakes)*

19	A	flutter	25	A	famin	31	A	senior
	B	wealthy		B	furnish		B	vicinity
	C	cereal		C	furious		C	dominoes
	D	gayge		D	fearless		D	vacume
	E	*(No mistakes)*		E	*(No mistakes)*		E	*(No mistakes)*

20	J	grammar	26	J	rural	32	J	candidate
	K	whitle		K	disagreed		K	absence
	L	presence		L	addhesive		L	conservation
	M	mashed		M	hydrant		M	register
	N	*(No mistakes)*		N	*(No mistakes)*		N	*(No mistakes)*

21	A	twilight	27	A	involve	33	A	item
	B	utensil		B	invoice		B	momentary
	C	stadium		C	inward		C	indent
	D	eskort		D	iodine		D	teksture
	E	*(No mistakes)*		E	*(No mistakes)*		E	*(No mistakes)*

22	J	elaborate	28	J	helmet	34	J	geography
	K	mereley		K	nugget		K	marjin
	L	national		L	democrattic		L	province
	M	premium		M	rotten		M	yield
	N	*(No mistakes)*		N	*(No mistakes)*		N	*(No mistakes)*

STOP

Level 11

73

SAY: **It is now time to stop. You have completed Test 3. Make sure that you have carefully filled in your answer spaces and have completely erased any stray marks. Then put your pencils down and close your books.**

After the test has been scored, review the questions and answer choices with students. If students are having difficulty, provide them with additional practice.

S1
A On the third saturday of each
B month during the summer,
C there is a carnival in our town.
D *(No mistakes)*

STOP

S2
J Dr Edminster was very
K pleased to hear about
L our healthy eating habits.
M *(No mistakes)*

STOP

For questions 1–11, darken the circle for the line that has a capitalization error. Darken the circle for *No mistakes* if there is no capitalization error.

1
A On May 17, 1990, Jim Henson
B died. he was the genius
C who created the Muppets.
D *(No mistakes)*

2
J Mr. and Mrs. Richmond
K always have an open
L house on Christmas Day.
M *(No mistakes)*

3
A David and Beth are Canadians.
B Their family moved here last
C year from British columbia.
D *(No mistakes)*

4
J The weatherman said, "if I
K were you, I would take along
L an umbrella today."
M *(No mistakes)*

5
A   932 West Avenue
B   Salt Lake city, UT 84103
C   September 19, 1995
D *(No mistakes)*

6
J Gemstones, USA
K Tucson, AZ 86020
L Dear store manager:
M *(No mistakes)*

7
A I just started a rock collection.
B Please send me a list of the
C different kinds of Quartz you sell.
D *(No mistakes)*

8
J Do you ship rocks by UPS?
K   Thank You,
L   Veronica Delgado
M *(No mistakes)*

9
A At the school plant sale,
B Suki bought an african
C violet for her grandmother.
D *(No mistakes)*

10
J The Audubon society is for
K people who enjoy birds. I
L definitely want to be a member!
M *(No mistakes)*

11
A Our new history teacher is from
B Canton, Ohio. She seems nice,
C and I think i'm going to like her.
D *(No mistakes)*

GO ON

Level 11

Test 4: Language Mechanics

Allow 15 minutes for this test.

SAY: **Turn to Test 4, Language Mechanics, on page 74.**

Check to see that all students find Test 4.

SAY: **In this test you will use your language skills to find errors in capitalization and punctuation. Look at S1. Read the lines carefully. Then darken the circle for the line that has an error in capitalization. Darken the circle for *No mistakes* if there is no capitalization error.**

Allow students time to find and mark their answer.

SAY: **You should have darkened the circle for *A* because days of the week are proper nouns and should begin with a capital letter.**

Check to see that all students have filled in the correct answer space. Ask students if they have any questions.

SAY: **Now look at S2. Read the lines carefully. Then darken the circle for the line that has a punctuation error. Darken the circle for *No mistakes* if there is no punctuation error.**

Allow students time to find and mark their answer.

SAY: **You should have darkened the circle for *J* because an abbreviation should be followed by a period.**

Check to see that all students have filled in the correct answer space. Ask students if they have any questions.

SAY: **Now you will finish the test on your own. Read the directions for each section carefully. Then do questions 1 through 24 just as we did the samples. Darken the circle for each correct answer. When you come to the words *GO ON* at the bottom of page 74, continue working on the next page. When you come to the word *STOP* at the bottom of page 75, put your pencils down. You have 15 minutes to complete the test. You may now begin.**

Allow students 15 minutes to find and mark their answers.

S1   A On the third saturday of each
      B month during the summer,
      C there is a carnival in our town.
      D *(No mistakes)*

STOP

S2   J Dr Edminster was very
      K pleased to hear about
      L our healthy eating habits.
      M *(No mistakes)*

STOP

For questions 1–11, darken the circle for the line that has a capitalization error. Darken the circle for *No mistakes* if there is no capitalization error.

1   A On May 17, 1990, Jim Henson
    B died. he was the genius
    C who created the Muppets.
    D *(No mistakes)*

2   J Mr. and Mrs. Richmond
    K always have an open
    L house on Christmas Day.
    M *(No mistakes)*

3   A David and Beth are Canadians.
    B Their family moved here last
    C year from British columbia.
    D *(No mistakes)*

4   J The weatherman said, "if I
    K were you, I would take along
    L an umbrella today."
    M *(No mistakes)*

5   A 932 West Avenue
    B Salt Lake city, UT 84103
    C September 19, 1995
    D *(No mistakes)*

6   J Gemstones, USA
    K Tucson, AZ 86020
    L Dear store manager:
    M *(No mistakes)*

7   A I just started a rock collection.
    B Please send me a list of the
    C different kinds of Quartz you sell.
    D *(No mistakes)*

8   J Do you ship rocks by UPS?
    K Thank You,
    L Veronica Delgado
    M *(No mistakes)*

9   A At the school plant sale,
    B Suki bought an african
    C violet for her grandmother.
    D *(No mistakes)*

10   J The Audubon society is for
     K people who enjoy birds. I
     L definitely want to be a member!
     M *(No mistakes)*

11   A Our new history teacher is from
     B Canton, Ohio. She seems nice,
     C and I think i'm going to like her.
     D *(No mistakes)*

GO ON

Level 11

74

For questions 12–24, darken the circle for the line that has a punctuation error. Darken the circle for *No mistakes* if there is no punctuation error.

12 J "Remember to take Scooter for
   K a walk as soon as you get home
   L from school today, said Dad.
   M *(No mistakes)*

13 A Clyde saw the movie,
   B *Jurassic Park* fifteen times
   C during his summer vacation.
   D *(No mistakes)*

14 J We get out of school at 2:30
   K in the afternoon. Every other
   L Friday we get out at 200.
   M *(No mistakes)*

15 A Does anyone know where
   B my glasses are I can't
   C find them anywhere.
   D *(No mistakes)*

16 J My mother told me that I
   K "should watch out for poison ivy"
   L in the back yard. She was right!
   M *(No mistakes)*

17 A The Rosemans dog was lost.
   B Joanne and Gayle searched all
   C over the neighborhood for it.
   D *(No mistakes)*

18 J Our teacher asked, "Can
   K anyone explain the difference
   L between nouns and verbs?
   M *(No mistakes)*

19 A Last year our baseball team
   B played well, but this year
   C nobody can hit the ball!
   D *(No mistakes)*

20 J The sun is very strong at noon.
   K We shouldnt sit outside at that
   L time without wearing sunscreen.
   M *(No mistakes)*

21 A   770 W. Areba
   B   Hershey, PA 17033
   C   October 16, 1995
   D *(No mistakes)*

22 J Penn. Central Fire Station
   K Philadelphia, PA 17609
   L Dear firefighters
   M *(No mistakes)*

23 A My club is interested in learning
   B more about fire safety? Could you
   C please send some information?
   D *(No mistakes)*

24 J We look forward to your reply.
   K   Sincerely,
   L   Ralph Doss
   M *(No mistakes)*

STOP

Level 11

75

SAY: **It is now time to stop. You have completed Test 4. Make sure that you have carefully filled in your answer spaces and have completely erased any stray marks. Then put your pencils down and close your books.**

After the test has been scored, review the questions and answer choices with students. If students are having difficulty, provide them with additional practice items.

Test 5: Language Expression

S1
A During the hurricane,
B the giant waves was
C crashing against the shore.
D (No mistakes)

STOP

For questions 1–12, darken the circle for the line that has an error in the way words are used. Darken the circle for *No mistakes* if all the words are used correctly.

1
A In the forty-yard dash,
B Carolyn beet everyone in
C her class by two seconds.
D (No mistakes)

2
J Dad and I watched people
K canoeing on the lake. Now
L him and I want to try it.
M (No mistakes)

3
A At the close of the school
B year, our principal told
C us to have a great summer.
D (No mistakes)

4
J The new brick mansion on the
K hill is more grander than any
L house Yoshi has ever seen.
M (No mistakes)

5
A Mari and her mom went to the
B library to borrow books so they
C might could read together.
D (No mistakes)

6
J After she slipped and felled
K in the stream, Celena's pants
L and shirt were soaking wet.
M (No mistakes)

7
A The feathers in Grandma's
B warm comforters that we use in
C the winter come from gooses.
D (No mistakes)

8
J The old house it burned to the
K ground very quickly. Luckily, no
L one was injured.
M (No mistakes)

9
A One of Jody's household chores
B are to water all of the house
C plants every Friday morning.
D (No mistakes)

10
J Shouldn't you ought to close
K the window before turning
L on the air conditioner?
M (No mistakes)

11
A The teacher said that Benny
B and I were the only two students
C who were not never absent.
D (No mistakes)

12
J Until that big brown bear started
K to chase us, I had never ran so
L fast in my life!
M (No mistakes)

GO ON

Level 11

Test 5: Language Expression

Allow 20 minutes for this test.

SAY: **Turn to Test 5, Language Expression, on page 76.**

Check to see that all students find Test 5.

SAY: **In this test you will use your language skills to find correct language expression. Look at S1. Read the answer choices carefully. Then darken the circle for the line that has an error in the way words are used. Darken the circle for *No mistakes* if all the words are used correctly.**

Allow students time to find and mark their answer.

SAY: **You should have darkened the circle for *B*. The subject, *waves*, is plural and requires a plural form of the verb. The verb should be *were*, not *was*.**

Check to see that all students have filled in the correct answer space. Ask students if they have any questions.

SAY: **Now you will finish the test on your own. Read the directions for each section carefully. Then do numbers 1 through 33 just as we did S1. Darken the circle for each correct answer. When you come to the words *GO ON* at the bottom of a page, continue working on the next page. When you come to the word *STOP* at the bottom of page 79, put your pencils down. You have 20 minutes to complete the test. You may now begin.**

Allow students 20 minutes to find and mark their answers.

For questions 13–22, darken the circle for the word or words that best fit in the underlined part of the sentence. Darken the circle for *No change* if the sentence is correct as it is.

13 Rodney cannot cross the street <u>though</u> his dad takes him.

A because

B unless

C than

D *(No change)*

14 We'll know the score <u>whether</u> the game is over.

J until

K when

L during

M *(No change)*

15 Is it wise <u>planning</u> for a rainy day and bring an umbrella?

A to plan

B by planning

C to have planned

D *(No change)*

16 David had to run <u>so that</u> he would not miss his bus.

J because

K while

L although

M *(No change)*

17 If you promise <u>returning</u> it, I will lend my camera to you.

A to return

B return

C will return

D *(No change)*

18 Now I can go to the park because I <u>having completed</u> my chores.

J was completing

K have completed

L completes

M *(No change)*

19 Fortunately there was nobody in the cave when something <u>explodes</u>.

A is exploding

B will explode

C exploded

D *(No change)*

20 If we leave out the cheese, maybe a mouse <u>will eat</u> it.

J is eating

K ate

L has eaten

M *(No change)*

21 Shopping has been easier <u>as</u> we moved to the city.

A before

B since

C where

D *(No change)*

22 If I wake up too early, I <u>have yawned</u> all day.

J will yawn

K was yawning

L had yawned

M *(No change)*

GO ON

For questions 23–26, read the paragraph. Then darken the circle for each correct answer. Darken the circle for *No change* if the sentence is correct.

> [1] For me, playing tennis is not as easy as it looks! [2] Have you ever played tennis? [3] Did you ever swing your racket at the ball and miss? [4] Many times, I have hit the ball right into the net. [5] My father has been practicing with me on weekends, but I don't seem to be getting any better. [6] I'm a much better volleyball player than tennis player. [7] Perhaps I hit the ball into the next court. [8] But worse than that is when the ball goes over the fence!

23 Choose the best way to write the underlined part of sentence 4.

A I have hit many times

B Many times, hitting, I have

C I have many times hit

D *(No change)*

24 What is the best way to write the underlined part of sentence 7?

J Sometimes L Carefully

K In the future M *(No change)*

25 What is the best concluding sentence to add to this paragraph?

A Would you like to play tennis with me sometime?

B I'm always hot and sweaty after playing a game of tennis.

C My dad just shakes his head and serves the ball again.

D It takes a lot of practice to learn to play tennis well.

26 Choose the sentence that does not belong in the paragraph.

J Sentence 1 L Sentence 5

K Sentence 2 M Sentence 6

For question 27, choose the answer that best fits the given situation.

27 Which would be most appropriate in a letter from a student to someone who has traveled in Africa?

A I hear you've been to Africa. What was it like? Do you have any pictures? Please send me information about your trip so I can do a social studies report.

B I understand you've recently been to Africa, and I wonder if I could interview you. I could come to your house on Saturday. That's really the only time that's convenient for me, so I hope we can meet then.

C I have to do oral research for a social studies project. If it is convenient, I would very much like to interview you about your recent trip to Africa. I hope you will be able to meet with me, as my schedule is flexible. I'm looking forward to talking with you soon!

D My teacher has given us a tough assignment. I need to interview you about your trip to Africa. I'll like to come to your house Saturday morning at ten o'clock.

GO ON

Level 11

78

For questions 28 –33, darken the circle for the sentence that expresses the idea most clearly.

28   J   Wearing the dime-store ring on her finger turned it green.

       K   When she wore the dime-store ring, her finger turned green.

       L   It turned green when she wore the dime-store ring on her finger.

       M   On her finger, the dime-store ring turned it green.

29   A   While cleaning her room, Alix found her lost necklace.

       B   Her lost necklace, while cleaning her room, was found by Alix.

       C   Cleaning her room, Alix found her necklace, which had been lost.

       D   Alix found her lost necklace during the time she was cleaning her room.

30   J   A day, in Maine are made one hundred million wooden toothpicks.

       K   In Maine are made one hundred million toothpicks a day. Wooden ones.

       L   One hundred million wooden toothpicks are made in Maine each day.

       M   In Maine are made one hundred million wooden toothpicks a day.

31   A   The very large bears did not scare the boys.

       B   Although the bears did not scare the boys, they were very large.

       C   Although very large, the boys were not afraid of the bears.

       D   The boys, although the bears were very large, were not scared.

32   J   Unlike other apes, gorillas don't climb trees like other apes.

       K   Other apes climb trees, but gorillas are not like them and don't.

       L   Gorillas are different from other apes because they don't climb trees and other apes do.

       M   Unlike other apes, gorillas do not climb trees.

33   A   Jason enjoying to ride his skateboard all over town.

       B   Enjoying riding his skateboard, Jason goes all over town.

       C   Jason enjoys riding his skateboard all over town.

       D   All over town, Jason enjoys riding his skateboard.

STOP

Level 11

79

SAY: **It is now time to stop. You have completed Test 5. Make sure that you have carefully filled in your answer spaces and have completely erased any stray marks. Then put your pencils down and close your books.**

After the test has been scored, review the questions and answer choices with students. If students are having difficulty, provide them with additional practice.

Test 6: Math Concepts and Estimation

S1 Which numeral has the greatest value?

| 6837 | 6783 | 3687 | 6378 | 8367 |

A 6837   C 8367
B 3687   D 6783

STOP

For questions 1–34, darken the circle for the correct answer.

1 What should replace the △ in the multiplication problem shown here?

A 9
B 8
C 7
D 6

$$
\begin{array}{r}
232 \\
\times 64 \\
\hline
928 \\
13\triangle 2 \\
\hline
14\square 48 \\
\end{array}
$$

2 What is the value of the 3 in 57.63?

J 3 tenths
K 3 ones
L 3 tens
M 3 hundredths

3 The figure shown here demonstrates that $\frac{2}{3}$ is the same as what number?

A $\frac{2}{6}$
B $\frac{4}{6}$
C $\frac{4}{8}$
D $\frac{6}{9}$

4 What is another name for twenty-eight thousand forty?

J 28,004   L 28,044
K 28,040   M 28,400

5 Ari is sixth in line for skating tickets. How many persons will buy tickets before he does?

A 3   C 5
B 4   D 6

6 What is another way to write fifty-three thousandths?

J 0.053   L 5.3
K 0.53   M 5300

7 What number is an even multiple of 6?

A 10   C 28
B 18   D 35

8 By how much does the value change if the 3 in 7328 is changed to a 9?

J 6   L 500
K 60   M 600

9 What fraction of the set of shapes are squares?

A $\frac{3}{8}$
B $\frac{3}{5}$
C $\frac{5}{8}$
D $\frac{8}{5}$

GO ON

Level 11

80

Test 6: Math Concepts and Estimation

Allow 25 minutes for this test.

Distribute scratch paper to students. Tell them they may use the scratch paper to work all problems except numbers 28 through 34 on page 83. These are estimation problems that students should work in their heads.

SAY: **Turn to Test 6, Math Concepts and Estimation, on page 80.**

Check to see that all students find Test 6.

SAY: **In this test you will use your mathematics skills to solve problems. Look at S1. Read the question silently, then darken the circle for the correct answer.**

Allow students time to find and mark their answer.

SAY: **You should have darkened the circle for *C* because *8367* is greater in value than any of the other numerals listed.**

Check to see that all students have filled in the correct answer space. Ask students if they have any questions.

SAY: **Now you will finish the test on your own. Read the directions carefully. Do numbers 1 through 34 just as we did S1. Darken the circle for each correct answer. When you come to the words *GO ON* at the bottom of a page, continue working on the next page. When you come to the word *STOP* at the bottom of page 83, put your pencils down. You have 25 minutes to complete the test. You may now begin.**

Allow students 25 minutes to find and mark their answers.

10 Which numeral has a value between 5364 and 6435?

J 4565   L 6543

K 5643   M 6634

11 Which symbol would replace the ○ in the following number sentence?

$$18 \bigcirc 2 = 3 \times 3$$

A +   C ×

B −   D ÷

12 How could the following number sentence be solved?

$$\square \div 7 = 28$$

J Add 28 and 7.

K Multiply 28 times 7.

L Subtract 7 from 28.

M Divide 28 by 7.

13 What would replace the □ to make the number sentence true?

$$(3 + 6) + 5 = (6 + \square) + 5$$

A 0   C 5

B 3   D 6

14 Which numeral will make this number sentence true?

$$(4 \times \square) + 5 = 21$$

J 4   L 6

K 5   M 7

15 If Larry picked one of the cards shown here without looking, which of the cards would he most likely pick?

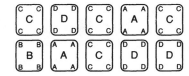

A A   C C

B B   D D

16 What is the average (mean) of this set of numbers {18, 11, 30, 29}?

J 11   L 22

K 18   M 29

17 Which set of numbers below has the greatest average (mean)?

A {11, 4, 12}   C {12, 7, 8}

B {12, 8, 2}   D {16, 4, 13}

18 Marty's favorite board game uses a spinner like the one shown here. **When Marty spins the spinner, on which number is the spinner most likely to stop?**

J 1
K 2
L 3
M 4

19 A white, a green, and a blue chip are in a box. **If the white chip is picked first, how many different ways can the other chips be picked?**

A 1   C 3
B 2   D 4

20 **Which picture shows parallel lines?**

J

L

K   M

21 The figure shown here has $\frac{8}{12}$ of its area shaded. **How much is <u>not</u> shaded?**

A $\frac{1}{2}$
B $\frac{1}{3}$
C $\frac{2}{3}$
D $\frac{3}{4}$

22 **One piece of the puzzle is missing. Which piece is the missing one?**

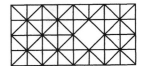

J   L

K   M

23 Mr. Ramirez's brick patio is in the shape of a rectangle. **How many feet of redwood fencing are needed to go around the entire patio?**

8 ft.

12 ft.

A 20 feet   C 80 feet
B 40 feet   D 96 feet

24 **Which unit of measurement is best to use to describe the weight of an egg?**

J Yards   L Liters
K Ounces   M Inches

25 **Which clock shows the time it will be in three and one-half hours, if it is 11:45 A.M. now?**

A 2:45 P.M.   C 3:15 P.M.
B 2:15 P.M.   D 2:30 P.M.

GO ON

Level 11

82

26 One quart is closest in value to which measurement?

J 1 kilogram   L 1 liter

K 1 pint   M 1 meter

27 Which figure below is a parallelogram?

 A

C

B

D

28 The closest estimate of 4213 + 5817 is _____.

J 4000 + 5000

K 4000 + 6000

L 5000 + 5000

M 5000 + 6000

29 The closest estimate of $18.98 − $7.38 is _____.

A $9   C $12

B $11   D $14

30 The closest estimate of the cost of 38 milk cartons is _____.

1 carton costs 39¢

J $0.39   L $16.00

K $0.80   M $19.00

31 The closest estimate of 55,432 ÷ 6 is _____.

A 90

B 900

C 9000

D 90,000

32 The closest estimate of 2109 ÷ 7 is between _____.

J 100 and 200

K 200 and 300

L 300 and 400

M 400 and 500

33 The closest estimate of the total cost of buying 5 magazines is _____.

OUTDOOR

ADVENTURES

Cost of 5 magazines

$4.00

$2.75

$4.50

$2.75

$2.75

A $14

B $15

C $18

D $20

34 The closest estimate of 461 × 736 is _____.

J 400 × 700

K 400 × 800

L 500 × 700

M 500 × 800

STOP

Level 11

83

SAY: **It is now time to stop. You have completed Test 6. Make sure that you have carefully filled in your answer spaces and have completely erased any stray marks. Then put your pencils down and close your books.**

After the test has been scored, review the questions and answer choices with students. If students are having difficulty, provide them with additional practice items.

Test 7: Math Problems

S1 Mark had 66 marbles to divide among 7 friends. **If each friend received the same number of marbles, how many marbles did Mark have left?**

A 2   C 9

B 3   D Not given

STOP

For questions 1–12, darken the circle for the correct answer. Darken the circle for <u>Not given</u> if the answer is not shown.

Use the table below to answer questions 1–3.

School Supplies	
Folder	$0.75
Markers	$2.50 pack
Glue	$0.75 stick
Notebook	$1.25
Pencils	$0.75 pack
Pens	$1.50 pack
Ruler	$0.50
Scissors	$3.25

1 What does 1 pack of markers, 1 notebook, 1 folder, and 1 stick of glue cost altogether?

A $3.25   C $5.25

B $4.75   D $5.75

2 How much change should Koji receive from $10.00 if he buys 1 ruler, a pair of scissors, 1 pack of pencils, and 1 pack of pens?

J $4.00   L $6.00

K $5.00   M $16.00

3 Grady needs 3 folders, a pair of scissors, and 2 sticks of glue. **How much money does he need?**

A $2.25   C $6.25

B $5.50   D Not given

4 A tree nursery had 5 rows of maple trees with 45 trees in each row. They received an order for 300 maple trees. **What can you conclude about the order?**

J The nursery would have 75 maple trees left.

K The nursery delivered 525 trees.

L The nursery needed 75 more maple trees.

M The nursery had exactly the number of trees ordered.

5 Neil and Donna picked 22 baskets of apples in their uncle's orchard. They plan on using 4 baskets to make applesauce and sharing the remaining baskets equally. **How many baskets will they each get?**

A 7   C 11

B 9   D 13

6 Mr. Yamada ordered 1,147 science books for the middle school. There were 248 books in the first shipment. **How many more science books still need to be delivered to Mr. Yamada?**

J 881

K 891

L 899

M Not given

GO ON

Level 11

Test 7: Math Problems

Allow 15 minutes for this test.

Distribute scratch paper to students. Tell them to compute their answers on the scratch paper.

SAY: **Turn to Test 7, Math Problems, on page 84.**

Check to see that all students find Test 7.

SAY: **In this test you will use your mathematics skills to solve problems. Look at S1. Read the problem silently, then darken the circle for the correct answer. Darken the circle for <u>Not given</u> if the answer is not shown.**

Allow students time to find and mark their answer.

SAY: **You should have darkened the circle for _B_ because 66 divided by 7 equals 9, with a remainder of _3_.**

Check to see that all students have filled in the correct answer space. Ask students if they have any questions.

SAY: **Now you will finish the test on your own. Read the directions carefully. Then do numbers 1 through 12 just as we did S1. Darken the circle for each correct answer. Darken the answer for <u>Not given</u> if the answer is not shown. When you come to the words _GO ON_ at the bottom of page 84, continue working on the next page. When you come to the word _STOP_ at the bottom of page 85, put your pencils down. You have 15 minutes to complete the test. You may now begin.**

Allow students 15 minutes to find and mark their answers.

Use the graph below to answer questions 7–9.

Number of Cars Sold in 1 Year

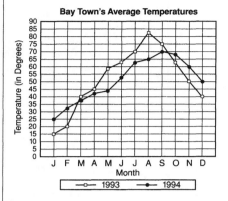

Each 🚗 =100 cars

7 Which dealership sold the most cars?

A Car City

B Downtown Motors

C Smith's Car Emporium

D Carver Car Sales

8 How many more cars were sold by Car City than by Smith's Car Emporium?

J 100   L 200

K 150   M 250

9 What was the average number of cars sold by the four dealerships in one year?

A 445   C 525

B 475   D 1,900

The graph below shows the average monthly temperatures for Bay Town for two years. Use the graph to answer questions 10–12.

Bay Town's Average Temperatures

10 What was the lowest temperature recorded in Bay Town during the two-year period?

J –20°   L 10°

K 5°   M 15°

11 Which month shows the greatest temperature difference between 1993 and 1994?

A December

B July

C August

D September

12 How many months in 1994 had an average temperature above 50°?

J 2   L 6

K 4   M 7

STOP

Level 11

85

SAY: **It is now time to stop. You have completed Test 7. Make sure that you have carefully filled in your answer spaces and have completely erased any stray marks. Then put your pencils down and close your books.**

After the test has been scored, review the questions and answer choices with students. If students are having difficulty, provide them with additional practice.

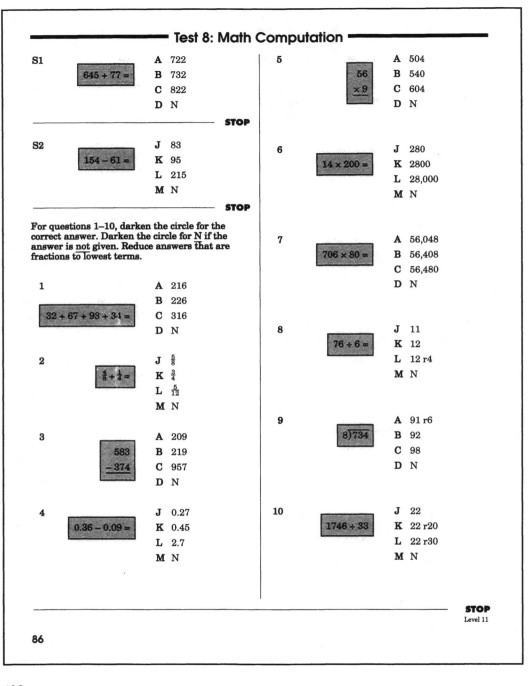

Test 8: Math Computation

Allow 10 minutes for this test. Distribute scratch paper to students. Tell them to compute their answers on the scratch paper.

SAY: **Turn to Test 8, Math Computation, on page 86.**

Check to see that all students find Test 8.

SAY: **In this test you will use your mathematics skills to solve problems. Look at S1. You are asked to add 645 and 77. Work the problem. Then darken the circle for the correct answer. If the correct answer is not given, darken the circle for N.**

Allow students time to find and mark their answer.

SAY: **You should have darkened the circle for A because 645 + 77 = 722.**

Check to see that all students have filled in the correct answer space.

SAY: **Now look at S2. You are asked to subtract 61 from 154. Work the problem. Then darken the circle for the correct answer. If the correct answer is not given, darken the circle for N.**

Allow students time to find and mark their answer.

SAY: **You should have darkened the circle for M because 154 – 61 = 93 and 93 is <u>not</u> one of the answer choices given.**

Check to see that all students have filled in the correct answer space.

SAY: **Now you will finish the test on your own. Read the directions carefully. Then do questions 1 through 10 just as we did the samples. Darken the circle for each correct answer. If the correct answer is not given, darken the circle for N. When you come to the word *STOP* at the bottom of page 86, put your pencils down. You have 10 minutes to complete the test. You may now begin.**

Allow students 10 minutes to find and mark their answers.

SAY: **It is now time to stop. You have completed Test 8. Make sure that you have carefully filled in your answer spaces and have completely erased any stray marks. Then put your pencils down and close your books.**

After the test has been scored, review the questions and answer choices with students. If students are having difficulty, provide them with additional practice.

S1

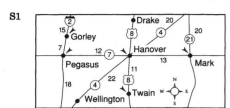

What city is located at the intersection of highways 7 and 8?

A Gorley

B Pegasus

C Hanover

D Mark

STOP

For questions 1–15, darken the circle for the correct answer.

Use the map below, which shows part of a city, to answer questions 1–4.

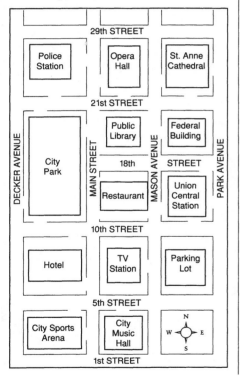

1 **Which is located on the east side of Mason Avenue?**

A The public library

B City Music Hall

C St. Anne's Cathedral

D City Sports Arena

2 **Which is located along Decker Avenue?**

J Opera Hall

K City Park

L The television station

M City Music Hall

3 **To go from the federal building to the television station, June walked**

A west, then north.

B east, then north.

C east, then south.

D west, then south.

4 **Which route did Ted take from Union Central Station to the hotel?**

J Park Avenue, then 29th Street

K 21st, then Decker Avenue

L 18th, then Park Avenue

M Mason, then 10th

GO ON

Level 11

87

Test 9: Maps and Diagrams

Allow 20 minutes for this test.

SAY: **Turn to Test 9, Maps and Diagrams, on page 87.**

Check to see that all students find Test 9.

SAY: **In this test you will use your study skills to interpret information in visual materials. Look at S1. Study the map carefully. Read the question silently, then darken the circle for the correct answer.**

Allow students time to find and mark their answer.

SAY: **You should have darkened the circle for *C* because the map shows that *Hanover* is located at the intersection of highways 7 and 8.**

Check to see that all students have filled in the correct answer space. Ask students if they have any questions.

SAY: **Now you will finish the test on your own. Read the directions carefully. Study the visual materials. Then do questions 1 through 15 just as we did S1. Darken the circle for each correct answer. When you come to the words *GO ON* at the bottom of a page, continue working on the next page. When you come to the word *STOP* at the bottom of page 89, put your pencils down. You have 20 minutes to complete the test. You may now begin.**

Allow students 20 minutes to find and mark their answers.

The maps show an imaginary country made up of four states. The top map shows resources and products. The bottom map shows major cities, rivers, and highways. Use these maps to answer questions 5–10.

Products/Resources Key

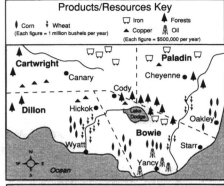

‡ Corn   ‡ Wheat
(Each figure = 1 million bushels per year)

⬓ Iron   ▲ Forests
▲ Copper   ⛏ Oil
(Each figure = $500,000 per year)

Political/Physical Map Key

| 0 | 250 | 500 | 1000 km |
| 0 | 250 | 500 | 1000 | 1500 miles |

● Major City
— Main Highway
- - - State Boundary

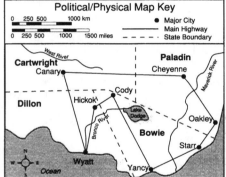

5 About how many miles is Yancy from Starr?

A About 500 miles

B About 750 miles

C About 1,000 miles

D About 1,500 miles

6 The economy of Oakley is most likely based on

J paper milling.

K fishing.

L steel production.

M agriculture.

7 What city is shown in this picture?

A Wyatt   C Starr

B Yancy   D Cody

8 If a bus went from Cody to Yancy, in which direction would it be traveling?

J Northwest   L Southwest

K Northeast   M Southeast

9 What is the value of copper produced each year in this country?

A $500,000   C $3,500,000

B $1,500,000   D $6,000,000

10 How much wheat is produced in Dillon each year?

J 2 million bushels

K 3 million bushels

L 4 million bushels

M 8 million bushels

GO ON
Level 11

88

After the test has been scored, review the questions and answer choices with students. If students are having difficulty, provide them with additional practice.

Use the following schedule to answer questions 11–13.

Pacific Islands Activity Center

Time	Fire Making, Coconut Husking and Coconut Tree Climbing	Handicrafts Demonstration	Bamboo Music/Dance Lesson	Island Tour Lecture	Hula Presentation	Weaving Demonstration	Cultural Presentation	Coconut Weaving	Songs and Dances
1:30									
1:35	◆								
1:45		◆	◆					◆	
2:00		◆		◆	◆	◆			
2:15		◆				◆		◆	
2:30				◆	◆				
2:35	◆	◆				◆			
2:45		◆	◆			◆			
3:00		◆		◆	◆	◆	◆		
3:15		◆					◆		
3:30				◆	◆				◆
3:35	◆	◆				◆		◆	
3:45		◆	◆			◆			
4:00		◆		◆	◆	◆	◆		
4:15		◆				◆		◆	
4:30				◆	◆				◆
4:35	◆	◆				◆		◆	
4:45		◆	◆			◆			
5:00			◆			◆	◆		

11 What demonstrations are offered at 2:00?

A Handicrafts, island lecture, hula, weaving demonstration

B Fire making, coconut husking, coconut weaving

C Bamboo music/dance, island lecture, cultural presentation

D Handicrafts, bamboo music/dance, coconut weaving

12 If Luke went to the island lecture at 2:00, what is the earliest time that he could see a weaving demonstration?

J 2:15 L 3:00

K 2:45 M 4:00

13 How many times is a handicraft demonstration presented in the Pacific Islands Center?

A 17

B 13

C 7

D 4

Use the following graph to answer questions 14 and 15.

Favorite Public Television Programs

Kind of Program	Women	Men	Teens	Children
British comedies	■■■■■■■■■■		■	
British mysteries	■■■■■■	■■■	■■	
Concerts	■■■	■■■■	■■■■■	■■
Plays, operas	■■■■	■■	■	
Science programs	■■	■■■	■■	■■■■
Nature programs	■■■	■■■		■■■■■
How-to programs	■■■ ■■■■	■■■■	■	
Travel programs	■■■■■	■■■■■	■■■	
Children's shows	■■	■	■	■■■■■ ■■■■■

Each ■ = 50 people

14 Which programs were most popular among teens?

J Concerts

K British mysteries

L Science programs

M How-to programs

15 How many women watched British comedies?

A 150

B 250

C 350

D 400

STOP

Level 11

89

Test 10: Reference Materials

Our Government

CONTENTS

S1 Which chapter might explain the Bill of Rights?

A Chapter 1
B Chapter 2
C Chapter 3
D Chapter 4

STOP

Use the table of contents in S1 to answer questions 1–4.

1 Which chapter might explain how the Supreme Court works?

A Chapter 1   C Chapter 3
B Chapter 2   D Chapter 4

2 On what page should you begin reading to learn about the parts of the Constitution?

J Page 2   L Page 36
K Page 21   M Page 84

3 Which chapter might discuss how Americans influence their government?

A Chapter 1   C Chapter 3
B Chapter 2   D Chapter 4

4 On what page should you begin reading to learn about James Madison's role in developing the Constitution?

J Page 2   L Page 36
K Page 21   M Page 84

For questions 5–10, choose the word or name from each group that would come first if the words or names were put in alphabetical order.

5
A mascot
B marvel
C marshal
D maroon

6
J graceful
K graduate
L grace
M gradual

7
A MacGruder, Colleen
B MacNulty, Carl
C McMurphy, Colin
D MacGraw, Clive

8
J saucer
K saturate
L saunter
M savory

9
A Toronto
B Toledo
C Towanda
D Topeka

10
J plasma
K plaque
L plaster
M plastic

GO ON

Level 11

Test 10: Reference Materials

Allow 20 minutes for this test.

SAY: **Turn to Test 10, Reference Materials, on page 90.**

Check to see that all students find Test 10.

SAY: **In this test you will use your study skills to identify reference sources and to locate and interpret information in them. Look at S1. Study the table of contents and read the question silently. Then darken the circle for the correct answer.**

Allow students time to find and mark their answer.

SAY: **You should have darkened the circle for *C*. The Bill of Rights are the first ten amendments to the Constitution and would most likely appear in a chapter about the Constitution.**

Check to see that all students have filled in the correct answer space. Ask students if they have any questions.

SAY: **Now you will finish the test on your own. Read the directions carefully. Then do numbers 1 through 24 just as we did S1. Darken the circle for each correct answer. When you come to the words *GO ON* at the bottom of a page, continue working on the next page. When you come to the word *STOP* at the bottom of page 92, put your pencils down. You have 20 minutes to complete the test. You may now begin.**

Allow students 20 minutes to find and mark their answers.

Use the set of encyclopedias shown here to answer questions 11–14.

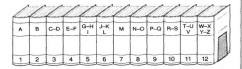

11 Which volume might have information about the six wives of King Henry VIII of England?

A Volume 4   C Volume 6

B Volume 5   D Volume 9

12 Which volume might describe the eating habits of bighorn sheep?

J Volume 1   L Volume 7

K Volume 3   M Volume 10

13 Which volume might explain how the Richter scale measures the force of earthquakes?

A Volume 3   C Volume 7

B Volume 5   D Volume 10

14 Which volume might describe Marco Polo's travels to China?

J Volume 3   L Volume 7

K Volume 4   M Volume 9

For questions 15–18, darken the circle for the correct answer.

15 Which of these sources would have information about the culture of the Pacific Islands?

A An almanac

B A dictionary

C An atlas

D An encyclopedia

16 Which topic would most likely be discussed in a health book?

J The contributions of Florence Nightingale

K Foods necessary for a healthy diet

L How furnaces work

M Wheat-growing regions in the United States

17 Which magazine would most likely discuss the latest medical research?

A *Reader's Digest*

B *Journal of the American Medical Association*

C *National Geographic*

D *CD Review*

18 Which would be found in an atlas?

J The latest baseball statistics

K The names of U.S. Presidents

L The activities of Congress

M The most direct route from Miami to New York City

GO ON

Use the sample dictionary and the pronunciation key to answer questions 19–22.

---

onus • ox

o•nus (ō´ nəs) *n.* A heavy or burdensome necessity, responsibility, or obligation.

o•paque (ō pāk´) *adj.* **1.** Not capable of letting light pass through: *Metals and some minerals are opaque.* **2.** Not reflecting light; not shiny; dull.

opener (ō´ pə nər) *n.* Something or someone that opens.

os•ten•ta•tious (os tən tā´ shəs) *adj.* Elaborately showy so as to impress others: *an ostentatious party.*

ox (oks) *n. pl.* **ox•en** (ok´ sən) An adult male of domestic cattle.

An ox

1. Pronunciation Key

a	at	o	hot	u̇	pull
ā	ape	ō	old	û	turn
ä	far	ô	song	ch	chin
â	care	ô	fork	ng	sing
e	end	oi	oil	sh	shop
ē	me	ou	out	th	thin
i	it	u	up	t̲h̲	this
ī	ice	ū	use	hw	in white
î	pierce	ü	rule	zh	in treasure

The ə symbol stands for the unstressed vowel heard in **about**, **taken**, **pencil**, **lemon**, and **circus**.

2. Abbreviations: *n.*, noun; *v.*, verb; *adj.*, adjective; *pl.*, plural.

---

19 What is the plural of the word *ox*?

   A oxes   **C** oxies

   B oxi   **D** oxen

20 Which syllable of *ostentatious* is accented?

   J The first   **L** The third

   K The second   **M** The fourth

21 How should the word that means "not reflecting light" be spelled?

   A opake   **C** opaqe

   B opaque   **D** opakue

22 The *u* in *onus* sounds like the

   J *a* in opaque.

   K *o* in opener.

   L *a* in ostentatious.

   M *e* in oxen.

Use the card from a library card catalog to answer questions 23 and 24.

GERMAN PLANES

722.43   Barker, Fredereich
       German Planes of World War II / by
       Fredereich Barker; photographs by
       Owen James.
       — New York City: Military Press,
       1989. 163 p.: ill.; 27 cm.

       1. German Planes 2. World War
       II I. Title

---

23 Who is Owen James?

   A The author of the book

   B The publisher of the book

   C The subject of the book

   D The photographer of the book

24 What is the title of this book?

   J Military Press

   K German Planes of World War II

   L Fredereich Barker

   M Photographs by Owen James

STOP

Level 11

SAY: **It is now time to stop. You have completed Test 10. Make sure that you have carefully filled in your answer spaces and have completely erased any stray marks. Then put your pencils down and close your books.**

After the test has been scored, review the question and answer choices with students. If students are having difficulty, provide them with additional practice.